The Stars Were Big and Bright

The United States Army Air Forces and Texas During World War II

By Thomas E. Alexander

State House Press
McMurry University
Abilene, Texas

Library of Congress Cataloging-in-Publication Data

Alexander, Thomas E., 1931-
    The Stars Were Big and Bright: the United States Army Air
      Forces and Texas During World War II / Thomas E. Alexander
    p.   cm.
    Includes bibliographical references and index.
    ISBN 1-57168-323-3 hardback
    ISBN 978-1-933337-27-2 paperback
    1. World War, 1939-1945--Aerial operations, American.
    2. United States. Army Air Forces--History.
    3. World War, 1939-1945--Texas.   4. Texas--History, Military.
    I. Title.
    D790.A783   2000   99-29958
    940.54'4973--dc21   CIP

State House Press
McMurry Station, Box 637
Abilene, TX 79697-0637
(325) 572-3974
(325) 572-3991 fax
www.mcwhiney.org/press

Distributed by Texas A&M University Press Consortium
1-800-826-8911 * www.tamu.edu/upress

Printed in the United States of America.

ISBN-13: 978-1-933337-27-2
ISBN-10: 1-933337-27-3

For Capy

"The stars at night
Are big and bright
(clap clap clap clap)
Deep in the heart of Texas"

Contents

LIST OF MAPS AND ILLUSTRATIONS

Maps

Acknowledgments

One of the many warm pleasures encountered while working on a book project such as this is the discovery that so many others share an interest in the subject being researched. Perhaps even more pleasant is the further discovery that nearly all of them are eager to contribute their assistance, support, and reminiscences to the project.

Scholars, librarians, museum curators, archivists, historians, and particularly the men and women who actually experienced the excitement and heartache of World War II were all most generous with both their time and cooperation as this book lurched its way toward completion. My particular thanks and admiration go to the veterans of what some of them now refer to as the "Battle of Texas, 1942–1945." The many thousands of miles of travel required to meet with these men and women and attend some of their reunions became more than worthwhile when the war stories started and the memories began to flow. As you may well know, pilots, and most aviators in general, often find it all but impossible to talk without using their hands a very great deal. It was therefore a real treat to watch the old flyers' eyes brighten as their hands began to simulate long-vanished aircraft while gleefully recalling near-misses over West Texas and rough landings that apparently were always just short of being controlled crashes. The years seemed to fall away with the telling of these tall and colorful tales, and the old pilots were, for a priceless moment or two, young once again, free to soar through Texas skies.

Perhaps just as riveting were the stories told by the widows of the fallen eagles. Their recollections of the hardships of military life and the shock of their introduction to the closed 1940s society of small-town Texas were at once both poignant and proud. What might have seemed bitter to these remarkable women fifty-odd years ago has now become sweet with the passing of time. Their experiences in wartime Texas are recalled as being a great adventure and to many of them, the most exciting one of their lives.

In every city and town visited in the course of preparing this text, collaborators and uncompensated research assistants all but miraculously appeared. In Pecos, Bill Davenport gave us a tour of what had once been Pecos Army Airfield. He also pointed out the few surviving buildings that had been moved into Pecos from the base at war's end, and he spoke with obvious pride about what the airfield had meant to the little town in the early 1940s. All of this previously unpublished wealth of information came from this ex-sailor who returned from the South Pacific in 1945 only to find that the army men had married nearly every eligible girl in Pecos.

In Sweetwater, Mrs. Franzas Cupp and her staff at the Pioneer Museum shared their knowledge of the WASPs of Avenger Field along with a treasure trove of rare photographs. Nancy Marshall Durr, of the Texas Woman's University in Denton, led us to even more vintage photographs of the WASPs at Avenger Field. Maj. Bennet B. Monde was willing to give his perspective on the overall history of Avenger Field, while the courteous staff at Sweetwater's public library gave good guidance to the library's collection of books about the WASP experience.

In Amarillo, Ron Russell of the English Field Air and Space Museum provided warm Panhandle hospitality along with great photographs and a copy of a rare unpublished history of Amarillo Army Airfield. His fellow air enthusiast, firefighter Dick Whiteley, unlocked the doors to a long-vacant Strategic Air Command alert post for us to visit and then topped off the day with a memorable tour of Amarillo Air Terminal's massive SAC-built runway in a vehicle that Dick clearly wishes were an F-15 fighter aircraft instead of a Chevy Suburban.

In East Texas, historians and history buffs alike were eager to talk about Majors Field and Greenville as it was fifty years ago. Vincent Leibowitz, director of the American Cotton Museum, is an avid collector of local history, while W. A. (Cap) Caplinder has been part of that history for nearly seven decades. His recollections of what happened when the big army airfield came to town provided a clear and unvarnished insight into the actual experience of the war coming to East Texas in 1942. The staff at the excellent W. Walworth Harrison Library in Greenville was most courteous and helpful, while Tom Jackson voluntarily chauffeured us around the old base site and pointed out the base's much appreciated historical marker.

In Waco, the research field was not quite as fertile as it was in Greenville, until Richard J. Veit surfaced at last. Dick is a student of the history of the homefront during World War II, and through his good graces, material about Waco Airfield and its impact on its host community soon began to flow.

At Randolph Field, history is an almost palpable thing. The air force base itself is impressive, and the very symbol of a well-run, highly efficient modern military operation, yet over it all hovers an aura of tradition and heritage. Bruce Ashcroft, an historian with Air Education and Training Command Headquarters, could not have been more helpful or more eager to share his vast knowledge of air history. Staff Sergeant Jason Axberg of the 12th Flying Training Wing Historian Office was also generous with both his time and his office's historical resources. In San Antonio proper, the Texas Collection staff of the city's huge enchilada-red public library was very helpful, as was Chris Floerke at the University of Texas Institute of Texan Cultures.

In Harlingen, Felix Chavez of that booming city's sparkling new library opened the doors to all that remains of the printed history of Harlingen Army Airfield. He was always willing to dig ever deeper to find more historical nuggets. John Houston, at Rio Hondo's Texas Air Museum, gave us access to its collection of artifacts from the old airfield.

Way out west in Ward County, only a skeleton of one hangar remains of the once mighty Pyote Army Airfield. In nearby Monahans, however, the Ward County Historical Commission's Archives Section keeps the memory of the long-dead base alive. Elizabeth Heath and her associate Jackie Youngblood offered enthusiastic support and a goldmine of pictures of the Rattlesnake Bomber Base. They went the extra mile to ensure that the history of "their" base was well-represented in this book. I hope that it is. Although she is no longer actively involved with her creation,

Lenora Price is to be forever thanked for establishing the Rattlesnake Bomber Base Museum in Pyote. Though difficult to find, the little museum contains a wealth of memorabilia of the old flying field, most of it collected by Jim Marks.

My gratitude goes to all of the above good folk who have made this book possible, but my very special thanks must go to the one person who made the greatest contribution of all. For nearly seven decades as a dedicated reader of the acknowledgment pages in countless books, I have often found it touching but curious that so many writers seem to feel compelled to give their final thanks to their spouses. After sharing thousands of miles and hundreds of hours with my wife in pursuit of the quest that this book became, I can now fully appreciate why such gratitude is so often richly deserved. For her many editorial contributions, consistently sage practical advice, and countless other reasons, *The Stars Were Big and Bright* is most sincerely dedicated to Capy.

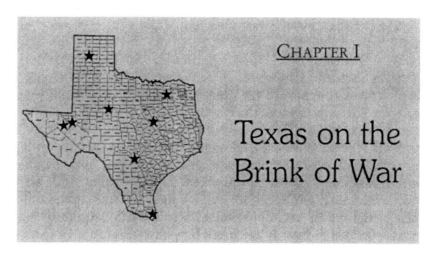

CHAPTER I

Texas on the Brink of War

For all its enormous range of space, climate, and physical appearance . . . Texas has a tight cohesiveness perhaps stronger than any other section of America.

John Steinbeck
Travels With Charley

When the celebrated American novelist John Steinbeck drove across Texas with his dog Charley in 1962, he was clearly struck by the sheer vastness of the place. The author also convinced himself that some sort of cementing bond, an almost impenetrable cohesiveness, held the whole sprawling state together despite its far-flung borders and its widely divergent cultures.

Steinbeck summed up his overall impressions in a simple phrase that through frequent usage has become something of an unofficial motto. "Texas," he observed, "is a state of mind."[1] Had the novelist made his journey only twenty years earlier, before World War II, he would have encountered a state that was even more cohesive, protective, and provincial than the one he and his poodle discovered in 1962. Perhaps Zane Grey, another American writer with a keen knack for turning a sharply perceptive phrase, had been close to the truth earlier when he wrote in 1936 that, "Texas was a world in itself."[2]

1

In late 1941, when America entered World War II, elements of great change, sudden and indelible, began to come to the Lone Star State. The unique world that for decades had been Texas was abruptly invaded by hundreds of thousands of American servicemen ordered to report to the many new military installations that had just been constructed. The newcomers brought with them what seemed to be almost alien social customs that were soon integrated into or, at least, superimposed upon long standing frontier traditions. Closed rural societies were gradually forced open by the arrival of soldiers in small towns where long sacrosanct social barriers were openly challenged for the first time. Countering this sudden disruption of traditional values was a much welcomed and equally sudden prosperity generated by a massive infusion of federal capital. Of the many agents of war-created change in Texas during World War II, perhaps the most significant was the United States Army Air Force.[*] Its nearly seventy wartime airfields were located all across the state with many of them situated near smaller towns where the social and economic impact of the base was particularly noticeable. The inhabitants of the state's larger cities, however, welcomed the freely flowing federal dollars every bit as eagerly as did their country cousins.

This book deals with eight army airfields that existed in Texas before, during, and occasionally after World War II. Each airfield was chosen for inclusion because there is something unique either about how it came into being, its mission, or what happened to it after the war ended. Amarillo, for example, was selected because its training program involved enlisted personnel rather than officers as was usually the case. Randolph Air Force Base was chosen because of its rich heritage and its continuing role in the nation's military flight training program. Avenger Field deserves inclusion because of its onetime status as the army's only all-female base, while other

---

[*]In June 1941, the official name of the army's air branch was changed from the Army Air Corps to the United States Army Air Forces. The new designation was used until September 18, 1947, when the U.S. Air Force was established as a separate service. During World War II, however, the air branch was commonly referred to as the U.S. Army Air Force, and for purposes of simplicity and grammatical expediency, this technically incorrect colloquialism will be used throughout this book.

fields are worthy of study primarily because they have simply disappeared. These huge and vital facilities, once vibrant in purpose and alive with dedicated people, are now only fading memories, for the most part unmarked and largely forgotten. Of the wartime bases included in this text, only Randolph Field still exists.

There are obvious parallels in the circumstances that were involved in the government's decision to place an army airfield near any given city, only to abruptly take it away when the time seemed right to do so. The partnerships that were forged between the cities and their airfields, however, were always unique and almost always mutually beneficial. The book is perhaps at most a series of thumbnail histories of the cities, the airfields, and some of the personnel who served there. It is punctuated with the reminiscences of those who shared the experience of Texas at war. They were eyewitnesses to a half-decade of significant change.

There can be no question that the opening of so many army airfields brought an immediate yet enduring change to the cloistered world that was Texas. If indeed it had been a world solely in itself prior to the war, the Lone Star State opened wide its gate to approximately one million uniformed visitors who most likely would have given little if any thought to becoming even temporary Texans had not the War Department sternly commanded them to do so.

What was it like, then, this sprawling and provincial Texas to which so many servicemen had suddenly found themselves transported? What made it so much different from any other state in a nation at war?

*As an old fella back in my hometown of Pittsburgh said to
me when he heard where I was going to be sent for training,
"Hell, Texas ain't nothin' but miles and miles of miles and
miles."*

Everett G. Slocum
New Braunfels, Texas
September 1998

Nearly everybody, including even most Yankees, knew that if
nothing else, Texas was undeniably huge and that the distances
between its borders were all but interminable. The largest in area of
all the United States at the time of World War II, it measures 814
miles from Beaumont on the east to El Paso on the west, and 872
miles from the top border of the Panhandle on the north down
south to Brownsville on the Rio Grande. In total, the state encom-
passes over 263,000 square miles making it larger than the combined land areas of Germany and Japan, America's two principal
foes in the war. Texas, for all of its vast size, was home to only six-
and-a-half-million people in 1940. This meant that there were only
about twenty-five people for each square mile of space, as compared
to the 272 New Yorkers who were crowded onto each square mile
of their home state at that same time.[3]

In addition to its often bragged about legendary size, Texas
was also widely known for its often extreme if not downright freakish weather conditions. The climate usually ranged from often very
cold winters in the north, complete with snow and ice, to a semi-
tropical paradise in the south where snow was unheard of and winter was more like summer. In between these two extremes were
mountains, deserts, prairies, and swamps, featuring, from time to
time, tornadoes, hurricanes, sand storms, blistering heat waves, and
numbingly cold blue northers. Even though people living outside of
Texas have always found it to be a less than interesting topic of con-
versation, the state also enjoys perfectly normal beautiful spring-
times and crisp autumn days.

In addition to the weather, visitors and residents of the state
also seemed inclined to talk abut its towering and limitless skies.
Travelers to the region since the beginning of its recorded history

had written their impressions of the almost overwhelming magnitude of those skies. Pedro de Castañeda de Náxera, who accompanied the Spanish explorer Francisco de Coronado on his long trek across what is now western Texas in 1541, wrote of being astounded by the phenomenon of "illimitable sky and earth."[4] United States Army Capt. Randolph Marcy, who explored the same region in 1855, made official note of the "sheer enormity of the sky."[5] According to many accounts, it was those vast skies that initially attracted army aviators to the state in the early 1900s.

The soldiers who arrived in such great numbers during World War II were obviously not the first military men to ever visit Texas. Army units of many nations had marched across the region for centuries. In addition to Coronado's *conquistadores* and Marcy's resourceful band of explorers, Mexican soldiers, Texian volunteers, Zachary Taylor's Mexican War Army of Occupation, and U.S. Cavalry troopers had ridden over and often died on Texas soil. During America's Civil War, the state that had only a short time before been a republic had cast its lot with the fledgling Confederate States of America, and although little in the way of actual fighting took place within the state's boundaries, some 127,000 Texans had marched along its roads on their way to fight for the futile Southern cause.

Following the defeat of the Confederacy in April 1865, victorious Union soldiers returned to Texas to enforce the harsh regulations of Reconstruction and to permanently remove Indians from the rapidly expanding Western Frontier. The overall departmental commander of those troops was the fiery little cavalryman, Philip H. Sheridan. Apparently not at all impressed with Texas or its skies, the general was openly unimpressed by its climate. On one memorable public occasion, he flatly declared that if he owned both Texas and hell, he would gladly live in the latter and rent out the former. In the time-honored manner of famous public figures before and since, Sheridan later retracted his biting words, claiming they had been taken out of context. At any rate, the soldiers serving in his command had no option but to endure whatever weather conditions came their way. When its post-Civil War tasks were finally completed, the army's presence in the state was relatively subdued for a time except for a brief flurry of recruiting and training activity in San Antonio at the beginning of the Spanish American War in 1898.

With the coming of World War I in 1917, however, the army

returned in force. The state proved to be an attractive location for training installations, with major camps being situated at Waco, El Paso, Houston, and particularly in San Antonio.

Military aviation, one of the most significant technological developments of the first world war, was in fact nurtured through its earliest years at Fort Sam Houston in the Alamo City. Shortly before that war, Lt. Benjamin Foulois, a self-taught and fearlessly reckless aviator, had brought the army's sole aeroplane to San Antonio in a determined effort to establish the nation's first military flying training center. The area had been selected primarily because of the relative flatness of its terrain, its usually balmy climate, and, as one historian suggests, "because Texas skies seemed to have been created just for flying."[6] This fortuitous early introduction of military aviation to San Antonio was a legacy that proved to be a major factor in shaping the role Texas would assume in World War II.

The years between the two great twentieth century wars brought about changes in the Lone Star State's demographics. Although the size of already large cities such as Dallas, Houston, and San Antonio increased rapidly, Texas continued to be largely an agricultural state, with nearly 70 percent of its population living in rural areas in 1920. Twenty years later, the national census of 1940 showed that despite the ongoing trend toward urbanization, over half of the state's residents still lived on farms or in small rural towns.[7]

The Texans of 1940, unknowingly poised on the brink of war, can be described in highly generalized but nevertheless statistically accurate terms. Nearly 86 percent of the population surveyed for that year's census were white, since many non-white residents were simply not counted. There were over thirty thousand more men than women despite the loss of the nearly four thousand soldiers who had been killed in World War I. Only a minority of all residents held a college degree and in many of the smaller communities, almost 60 percent of the adults over age twenty-five had not completed their high school education.[8]

Most men worked in agricultural occupations of some sort, while nearly all women worked in the home. The state's farms and ranches led the nation in the output of such diverse crops as cotton, cattle, pecans, goats, onions, and roses. Close behind agriculture in importance was the petroleum industry, but the dramatic surge in oil production was not to come until the thousands of new machines of war would require literally oceans of sweet Texas crude.

Most Texans did not have much need for their state's petroleum products for their own personal use in the years just before World War II. In 1938, only one of every five residents owned an automobile even though the state did proudly boast of its 15,000 miles of excellent hard-surfaced roadways over which those 1.2 million vehicles could be driven in relatively uncongested ease. Railroads, too, were an important mode of transportation before and during the war. By 1940, over seventeen thousand miles of railroad track criss-crossed the state. Indeed, the existence of such a well-developed highway and railway infrastructure was another significant factor in Texas's vital role as a leader in military activities during World War II.[9]

Before that war came, however, most Texans stayed close to their rural homes in relative isolation, despite the miles of railways and the traffic-free system of highways available to them. There were, of course, no television sets in their homes and only one million radios were to be found in the entire state in 1940, although surprisingly there were forty-one radio stations engaged in broadcasting at the time. Of the 693,323 telephones then in use, fewer than half were located outside the state's fifteen larger urban centers.

In the closely knit Texas communities, churches were an important aspect of pre-war life. One of every three Texans belonged to a church organization, all of which as might be expected placed great importance on long-held moral and spiritual values. The largest religious denomination was Baptist, with over 750,000 members or about 35 percent of the state's church goers. Another 500,000 worshipped at Roman Catholic churches.[10]

So these, then, were the statistically typical Texans whom the servicemen coming to the state would encounter. Loyal to their churches and their communities, they clung to traditional family values and were seemingly content, or perhaps obliged, to stay in their relatively remote world. Mostly rural residents, the average pre-war Texan seldom moved far from the place of his birth, living out his life to a large degree isolated, either by choice or circumstance. Most people in the smaller communities learned of national and international events mainly through reading their weekly newspapers or by watching the highly edited newsreels shown at the local movie houses.

In addition to all of their traditions and their long standing way of life, many of the state's residents also bore the burden of poverty in the years immediately before the war. The great economic depression that had brought financial devastation to other parts of the nation beginning in 1929 had impacted Texas somewhat belatedly but no less certainly. With unemployment rampant and with national demand for its many agricultural products declining at an alarming and disastrous rate, the economic outlook for the entire state was bleak at best. Faced with mounting personal financial difficulties and perhaps feeling somewhat anchored by the heavy chains of lingering nineteenth century traditions, even the most provincial of Texans could perhaps be forgiven for hoping, if not praying, for better economic times and a providential change in the routine and often downright monotonous pattern of his rural existence.

When aircraft of the Imperial Japanese Navy attacked Pearl Harbor, Hawaii, on Sunday, December 7, 1941, any and all prayers that might have asked for a change in long established ways of life were abruptly and grimly answered. For all Texans, as for all Americans, what President Franklin D. Roosevelt had called a day of infamy also proved to be the herald of years of profound and largely irreversible change.

The nation was now at war. Even though its long-anticipated entry into the conflict had been surprisingly sudden on that fateful Sunday morning, the United States had actually been preparing for it for several years. As early as 1938, officials of the Civil Aeronautics Administration (CAA) had been conducting a comprehensive survey of the nation's existing airport facilities and potential airport sites. Although rather thinly disguised as a strictly civilian endeavor, it was widely recognized that the actual purpose of the CAA survey was to identify and evaluate those key civilian air facilities that could be readily converted into Army Air Force flight training installations once the expected war started, or at least seemed imminently likely to do so. In all, 191 existing airports and potential sites were surveyed by CAA officials from 1938 through 1941, and 149 of these were ultimately selected for either massive expansion or new construction. Of all the airports or new sites finally chosen, almost half were located in Texas.

There were many political, climatic, natural, and economic reasons why the Lone Star State had scored so highly on the CAA survey, garnering perhaps a disproportionate share of the federal dollars that had been newly appropriated for air facility construction. Among them were its well-developed transportation infrastructure, its excellent interstate railway connections, and its location close to the geographical center of the nation. Other significant factors included direct maritime access to the state through its all-important seaports on the Gulf of Mexico and, of course, the apparently inexhaustible supply of regionally produced petroleum products.

Ironically, its often popularly much-maligned climate also helped tip the scales in favor of Texas. Meteorological studies had indicated that despite some highly publicized violent weather events, the state did in fact offer an unusually high number of clear days ideally suited for flight training. Further, low average annual rainfall amounts, particularly in the western part of the state, might periodically spell ruination to the area's farmers and ranchers, but the dry climate held ample promise that training schedules would seldom be interrupted by cloudy or stormy skies.

The legendary wide-open spaces of the plains and prairies also impressed the CAA officials. There were few looming mountain peaks to dangerously impede the forward progress of the fledgling pilot-trainees. According to one contemporary government statistic, Texas afforded "77,391,536 acres of treeless hills and plains" over which neophyte aviators could hone their flying skills and eventually perhaps earn their silver wings. Before the war came to its conclusion in 1945, the army's Air Training Command exercised direct control over nearly one million of those treeless acres.[11]

According to the CAA survey, Texas did have an impressively large number of existing air facilities of various sizes that could likely be leased by the War Department for development as military airfields when the time was appropriate to do so. Runways could obviously be lengthened, thickened, and widened far more economically than completely new airfields could be constructed. In pre-war America, despite the increasingly ominous prospects for a major worldwide conflict, military budgets were still comparatively limited. As the signs of war grew even more unmistakable, however, all such observances of federal fiscal conservatism gave way to a near-frenzied rush to expand or build airfields and to do so in great haste with little concern for the often excessive cost overruns that were likely to be incurred.

Texas cities, large and small, were enthusiastically eager to have the CAA survey teams favorably consider their communities as candidates for government-financed airport construction projects. The state's powerful political representatives in the nation's capital brought their formidable influence to bear on officials of both the CAA and the War Department in a concentrated effort to gain for their congressional districts much needed construction jobs at new or greatly enhanced air facilities. City leaders lent their considerable political weight to the effort, with mayors, councilmen, chambers of commerce, and even Rotary Clubs uniting in well-orchestrated campaigns to convince federal officials that their individual city was unquestionably the best qualified of all the hundreds of communities nationwide which were clamoring to be awarded the airfield contracts.

When President Roosevelt issued a directive calling for an additional 50,000 military aircraft and 30,000 pilots to fly them in view of the clearly impending national emergency, the search for airfields that could adequately provide the necessary training for the new aviators was expedited and promptly completed. The dedicated efforts of the Texas politicians and civic leaders proved to have been highly effective, and soon nearly seventy of the newly approved airfields were being built in the Lone Star State. Even before the war had started and with the bases far from completed, the vanguard of the well-over 200,000 Air Force trainees who would eventually serve in the state began to arrive. As a result, the population began to rapidly increase, growing at a faster rate during the first two years of the war than it had in the ten years between 1930 and 1940.[12]

This sudden growth gradually brought an end to the economic stagnation of the Great Depression. Over 500,000 Texans left their rural or small town homes, many for the first time in their lives, to take defense jobs in the larger metropolitan areas, while another 750,000 joined the nation's armed forces.[13] The extensive military construction projects gave well-paying employment to thousands who until recently had been out of work for months or perhaps even years. Newly expanded road crews worked twenty-four-hour shifts to bring the state's highways up to military standards, oil field and refinery employment levels increased rapidly, and the towns close to the newly opened airfields grew and prospered because of huge army payrolls. Texas, clearly at war, was experiencing an economic boom unlike any in its history.

However, the desperately needed and warmly welcomed financial recovery that swept across the state during the war also created many less than desirable social side effects, particularly in those cities and towns situated near the new army airfields. Housing was woefully inadequate in nearly all of the small communities, causing real estate prices and rents to soar well beyond the reach of many families. Food shortages and black market activities occurred, made even worse by the often baffling rationing programs put in effect by the government.

The coming of war and the concomitant opening of military facilities all across Texas gave rise to a sudden awareness of the need for stringent security precautions. Highway maps drawn during the war years did not divulge the locations of new military installations, and long established air bases were removed. An official state highway map of eastern Bexar County issued in 1945, for example, shows only a large blank space where the huge Randolph Field facility had previously been shown. Roadways leading into the blank space were retained up to a point and then abruptly terminated without explanation. Unless he was fortunate enough to possess an older, unaltered map, an enemy saboteur presumably would have found it difficult to even locate the two-thousand-acre Randolph Field installation, let alone damage it in some way.

The large and constantly expanding military population of the new airfields quite often exceeded that of the nearby towns. Soldiers on weekend passes usually outnumbered any locals who might venture out on a Friday or Saturday night. Prostitution, virtually unheard of in the smaller communities before the war, became a lucrative vocation, or in some cases, avocation. Even though many parts of Texas still observed various degrees of legal prohibition when the war started, contraband alcoholic beverages were made easily available to bored and thirsty soldiers by countless enterprising bootleggers.

Naturally enough, many of the young servicemen found the

local girls living in the nearby cities to be attractive, and their efforts to socialize with them often incurred the displeasure of the young ladies' parents. In some high schools, girls who dated soldiers from the airfields promptly found themselves blacklisted and ostracized by the male students.

The commanding officers of the various airfields made valiant efforts to control their high-spirited and frequently restless soldiers, and worked closely with civic and church leaders to prevent, or at least minimize, the disruption of the community's pre-war moral and social standards. As further insurance, however, military police patrols were often on duty in case matters grew seriously out of hand.

The civilians of Texas, patriotic to the core, for the most part warmly welcomed the military personnel into their previously tightly knit world, but with a tacit proviso that the servicemen at least attempt to behave themselves with reasonable restraint. If any personnel were inclined to misbehave, it was commonly held that they should do so in such a way that the misdeed could be conveniently ignored, at least if it was not too outrageous. Many people who then resided in what were known as army towns can still recall that the local citizenry accepted the servicemen and made every effort to overlook their transgressions for the simple reason that the opening of the nearby airfield had, for all intents and purposes, brought an end to the poverty and despair that had plagued the depression years immediately before the war. The prevailing attitude of the citizens living near the airfields seems to have been a heady mix of gratitude and forbearance wrapped in patriotism and a heartfelt pride that their town had an army installation of its very own right next door. According to one old-timer who remembers the war years clearly, this surprisingly benign attitude allowed miscreant soldiers "to get away with murder just so long as nobody got hurt."[14]

Despite the many diverse social pressures created during the war, the airfields themselves proved to be mutually beneficial to the Army Air Force and the cities located near the bases. The communities prospered and gained a large government-financed air facility that would in all likelihood be converted into a modern municipal airport after the war. The towns had also been exposed to new and enlightening perspectives on social values. Many traditional barriers to racial and gender equality had been repeatedly tested, evaluated, and often shaken if not altogether breached. On the other side of the equation, the Army Air Force discovered that it had found exactly the right locale to effectively train its aviators so that they could, in time, help win the war. In total, 45,000 pilots, 13,000 navigators, 12,000 bombardiers, 45,250 aerial gunners, and 74,000 aircraft mechanics graduated from training facilities located in Texas.[15]

It is possible that the Roosevelt administration itself benefited the most from its ambitious airfield building project, particularly before the war actually started. By cleverly using the universally popular promise of economic recovery as a lever, the administration was able to roll away large scale opposition to its defense build-up, which was viewed by many isolationists as clear evidence of President Roosevelt's intention to involve America in a foreign war. In short, the realization that new airfield construction would bring forth a flood of federal dollars into the stagnant Texas economy was powerful enough to erode both opposition to the nation's ever accelerating slide toward full scale participation in the war, and concerns about a major adjustment in the social status quo brought about by the sudden arrival of a multitude of strangers. The basic desire for economic survival served to fuel patriotism and markedly diminish the often fearful prospect of social change.

When the military airfields finally became fully operational, the previously tranquil skies over Texas seemed to be constantly alive with army aircraft of all types. During one record shattering eighteen-month-long marathon of flying, over eleven million hours of training time were logged. The wing tips and the fuselages of every aircraft were proudly emblazoned with the distinctive bright white star emblem of the United States Army Air Force. Day and night throughout the long war, those big and bright stars filled the vast Texas skies. Memories of them linger still.

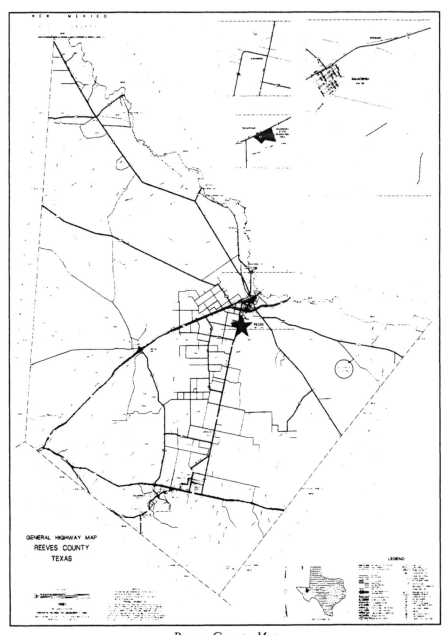

Reeves County Map
This map of eastern Reeves County shows the location of Pecos Army
Airfield during the war years. An inset map of Texas shows the location of
the county within the state.

CHAPTER II

Pecos and Pecos Army Airfield

What I remember most about Texas is that it was just very hot and almost empty. That, and the sky . . . I'd never seen anything like that great big sky before and I sure haven't seen anything like it in the fifty years since.

Richard E. Gilliam
New York City
May 1998

The United States Army, with its legendary and typically capricious whim of iron, had seen fit to order Aviation Cadet Richard Eugene Gilliam to report for duty at Pecos Army Airfield in the very middle of one of the hottest summers on record. It had taken nearly a week for the eighteen-year-old New Yorker to make the train trip from the relatively cool East Coast to the sun-baked plains of West Texas. At last, on 21 July 1943, at 0500 hours, as the army insisted such data be written, Gilliam and seventeen other young potential pilots stumbled off the stifling train to climb aboard the truck that would carry them to the airfield and the beginning of what they fervently hoped would be glorious careers as army aviators.

"I recall thinking that what I was barely able to see from the truck's headlights and the dim little street lamps might possibly look even worse when the sun came up," Gilliam remembered many years later, "and God knows it was grim enough even in the faintest of light. Sure enough though, when the sun finally did hit it full bore, the scene was just plain awful."[1]

As the truck roared through the all but deserted streets on its way to the airfield, Gilliam could see only nondescript clapboard houses scattered about on the sandy and treeless landscape. As the dawn gave way to daylight, an already hot southerly wind grew stronger, causing eddies of dust and sand to dance across the table-flat terrain. The sun that melted away the nighttime darkness, and seemingly everything it touched that summer morning, climbed rapidly and soon became a blazing red-orange disk. It was unobstructed by clouds or mountains and appeared even angrier looking because of the thin veils of dust that filled the sky. The heat that Gilliam and his fellow travelers had found to be all but suffocating in the pre-dawn darkness at the train station now became almost a living thing. The truck's driver shouted back to them that it was on its way to becoming another typical Pecos summer day with the temperature reading well over 100°. "This'll make twenty-two days in a row," he reported with obvious glee. "Welcome to Texas, y'all."

Reunion Stirs Memories Of Air Field Vets

> Headline
> *Pecos Enterprise*
> October 8, 1998

Although the handful of veterans who came back to Pecos for their reunion in the fall of 1998 had markedly changed from the fading fifty-year-old photographs taken of them when they were World War II cadets or instructors, it was obvious that much in the little West Texas town was still as it had been in the 1940s. Even though what was generally expected to be the final reunion for these ex-airmen who had served at Pecos Army Airfield took place in October, the thermometer reading nevertheless hovered around a very summer-like 105°. The wind still blew constantly, and stinging particles of sand and dirt filled the air. Above the thin clouds of dust, the seemingly limitless sky was as startlingly blue as the old pilots remembered it being so long before, but the sprawling airfield where they had learned to fly had virtually disappeared. Its nearly 2,000 acres, once alive with an almost electric vitality, had again become the domain of the rattlesnake and the sagebrush.

No signs nor markers could be found to inform visitors about the great wartime flight training base that for three years had flourished on this vast expanse of land. The old veterans, of course, had their memories of what Pecos Field was like in its days of glory, and a few of the townspeople still remembered how their lives were affected by the coming of the army to their depression-ravaged little town. To many of them, the opening of the air base and the economic revival it had triggered is now recalled as being one of the very best things that ever happened in the relatively short and violent history of Pecos, Texas.

THE CROSSROADS OF WEST TEXAS

Pecos is located some two hundred dusty miles east of El Paso. It draws its name but not its water from the nearby highly alkaline Pecos River. The town was established in 1881 and named the county seat of Reeves County in 1884. The site's proximity to the river caused it to become a confluence of many wagon and cattle trails for several years before the community was established. The Goodnight-Loving Trail and the Butterfield-Overland Stage Route had both found their way to the Pecos River, even though its water was usually not fit for either human or animal consumption. As one trailhand said of the river, "It ain't nothin' else, but at least it's wet."[2] In hot, dry, and dusty West Texas, just being wet has always accounted for a lot.

In the early 1880s, the Texas and Pacific Railroad arrived in tiny Pecos, affording the many large ranches that had been established in the region a new and comparatively economical way to ship their cattle to market. As was nearly always the case, the coming of the railroad also prompted the opening of numerous saloons in the small community. The cowboys driving their herds to the railhead were frequent and usually highly enthusiastic patrons of the saloons, with brawls, shootings, and murders being almost everyday occurrences in the town's early years.

The infamous outlaw Clay Allison took up a semi-permanent residence in one of the more notorious saloons. Although he was accused of several murders, the Pecos Chamber of Commerce insists that Allison never killed a man who didn't deserve being killed. Although some historians contend that Allison himself perhaps deserved to be shot, his death was actually caused by an accidental fall from a wagon at his ranch near Pecos in 1887. He was buried in the town cemetery, but in 1975 his remains were exhumed and reinterred in a grave in downtown Pecos near the Chamber of Commerce office, presumably for the convenience of tourists.

In time, the railroad-saloon-cowboy era of violence subsided and Pecos took on a somewhat more civilized appearance. By 1901, there were two schools with 148 pupils and four teachers, and in 1904, a bank opened to handle the financial needs of the town's population of just over 600 citizens. By 1931, there were 145 businesses in operation, but by 1933, America's great economic depression had caused that number to shrink to 110. The future of the little community near the Pecos River was anything but bright as the decade of the forties drew near.[3]

PECOS ARMY AIRFIELD

You'd have to admit that the Army came to our rescue right before World War II, just like the cavalry used to back in the Indian days.

J. R. Hennigan
Odessa, Texas
October 1998

As a longtime resident of Reeves County put it, "The establishment of this Army Flying School at Pecos was probably the most exciting segment of Pecos history."[4] Although the headline of the September 11, 1942, edition of the *Pecos Enterprise* claimed that "Pecos Didn't Bid For Flying School But Was Ready," other sources indicate that the city had in fact aggressively pursued a new air base for years.[5] According to the *New Handbook of Texas*, the city raised $10,000 through a bond issue in 1940 to expand its municipal airport. Likely aware of the rapid escalation of the war in Europe, the city council used some of the newly raised funds to acquire an additional four hundred acres of land adjacent to the still only rarely used airport facility. The balance of the bond money was used to clear, grade, and fence the new acreage. When that work was completed, the land then remained vacant, awaiting the eventual world event that would activate its use.[6]

Shortly before America's entry into World War II in December 1941, Pecos's city leaders repeatedly called the army's attention to the community's airport and its existing runways surrounded by the four hundred acres of highly potential land that was already conveniently prepared for construction. There is nothing in the Reeves County official history book to suggest that there was anything altruistic in the town's desire for a military installation. What Pecos asked from its federal government, according to the official account was ". . . just anything to provide a payroll."[7]

Only a few days after the Japanese attack on Pearl Harbor, the army sent a site survey team to Pecos to assess the municipal airport's suitability as a flight training base. The army's visit was supposed to be a secret, with knowledge of it to be shared only by the military investigators themselves and the Pecos Chamber of Commerce. It is difficult to believe, however, that by the time the army surveyors had left town after their short visit, all but perhaps a few of Pecos's 4,855 citizens knew what was afoot. Those who somehow might have missed out on the news of the secret visit had their eyes opened on December 19, 1941, when the local newspaper rather giddily announced, "Pecos Is Considered For Flying School."[8]

Rumors swirled throughout the region that the new flight installation would bring some 4,500 soldiers to Pecos, in effect doubling the town's population virtually overnight. Optimism and enthusiasm ran high as the city fathers imagined what such an increase in population would mean to Pecos's withered economy. The army, however, deferred any action, ever mindful of the effects of the land speculation that somehow always seemed to occur when new military installations were in the offing. As the days passed without word from Washington, the local businessmen grew increasingly concerned.

At last, on January 23, 1942, two more Army Air Force officers arrived in Pecos to conduct further site surveys. Obviously pleased with what they found, the officers gave the city council a lease agreement to be signed on the condition that an additional 320 acres of land adjacent to the airport could be acquired.

One week later, yet another army delegation descended on Pecos for what proved to be the final site investigation. After blithely advising the city's officials that an additional 1,800 acres would now be required for the 7,000-foot runways that were being planned, the officers departed. Once again, the city leaders were allowed to writhe in anticipation as the federal government went about its often nerve-wracking process of deliberation. Perhaps toying with Pecos, the War Department announced to the press on February 27, 1942, that a preliminary contract had been let for construction of a major "undisclosed West Texas project."[9] Pecos, of course, presumed that their so frequently inspected and well-researched air base site was to be the War Department's undisclosed West Texas project.

Taking no chances that it had failed to live up to its part of the agreement, the Pecos City Council called for another bond election on March 13, 1942. The proceeds from these bonds, which were rapidly snapped up by area investors, were used to acquire the additional land the army had recently indicated it would need for its airfield.

Just two weeks after this $50,000 bond issue had been successfully launched, the War Department officially announced that Pecos, Texas, was indeed to be the location of one of five new pilot training bases to be built immediately. The city reacted to the news with great jubilation, especially when the War Department further announced that the construction costs of the facility would be in excess of $5 million. According to the 1939 *Texas Almanac*, the total valuation of all property and improvements in Reeves County at the time was only $9,620,702. Pecos's far sighted pump-priming $10,000 bond issue earlier in September of 1941 was apparently going to increase the entire county's worth by over 50 percent.[10]

A government-built high wooden fence promptly appeared around that part of the 1,834-acre site that would soon have buildings constructed upon it, and security was tight. One longtime resident recently recalled that when she and her young child went to the base construction site to see her husband, who was working there, she was denied entry. Her child found this to be very disappointing, and his mother, trying to explain why they could not see Daddy, tried to make light of the situation, turning it into a game of spy for the child. He was soon heard excitedly exclaiming to his friends, "Me spy! Me spy!"[11]

Within a week after the major construction contract had been signed, over three hundred laborers were at work around the clock. The influx of workers touched off a housing crisis in Pecos that was to plague the city for as long as the airfield existed. The federal government found it necessary to impose rent ceiling restrictions in a town that only a few weeks earlier had had far more empty houses, apartments, and rooms than it had renters.

Building continued at a feverish pace on the airfield and, as was almost always the case, construction costs spiraled upward, well beyond the government's earlier estimates. An indication of how excessive the building costs had become is evident in the War Department's surprising announcement early in June 1942 that a flying school was to be built in Pecos at a cost of more than $3 million. Naturally enough, it was at once assumed by the community that a *second* flying field was going to be built close by, but it soon developed that the announcement was merely the War Department's way of appropriating an extra $3 million or so in order to absorb the massive cost overruns incurred at the Pecos facility that was already under construction. There would not be two bases after all, just one base for the price of two.[12]

Until permanent housing could be built, personnel arriving at the airfield lived in tents which offered little protection from the often extreme climatic elements, or from the rattlesnakes, the original occupants of not only the Pecos site, but of all West Texas as well. The snakes presented a daunting and dangerous problem, particularly during the brush clearing phase of construction. Rattlesnake killing became both a sport and a means of survival, with the day's body count often reported in terms of numbers of barrels-full of dead snakes rather than in individual reptiles dispatched. One cadet, Wilbur L. (Wib) Clingan, remembered that the killing of rattlesnakes was offered in lieu of the customary physical training classes.[13]

Although she admittedly loathed the lethal diamondback rattlers, Lucy Rountree Kuykendall, an officer's wife, seemed to be almost equally at odds with West Texas's often harsh weather. "We arrived in Pecos when the [flying] school was a tent city," she wrote just after the war, "a tent city wallowing in dust, soon to be mired in mud, for Pecos always did things superlatively."[14]

Other newcomers also bemoaned the weather conditions that they encountered. Ariel F. Bean, Class 44-F, remarked that at Pecos he slept on colored sheets for the first time in his life. When the laundry on the base was out of commission for over two months, Bean and his barrack-mates had to use the same sheets night after night. "The combination of red Texas dust and body sweat colored the sheets red," he remembered. Bean also recalled that the heat, dust, or mud were so bad that even the native Texans in his outfit found them hard to take. "One of the great advantages of being sent to Pecos," Bean wrote after the war, "was that after a couple of weeks no more was ever heard about how great a state Texas was. Some of the Texans present vocally willed that part of the state back to the Indians."[15]

With the snake population at least somewhat reduced and the erratic climate only grudgingly accepted, the base gradually settled into its projected role as one of America's largest pilot training facilities. By September 1942, just six months after the official announcement of the base had been released, the first class of one hundred cadets began flying from it. Meanwhile, construction work continued, with at least 1,500 men putting the finishing touches on the airfield's permanent buildings. At its peak, there were nearly 5,000 people working at the base, including over six hundred civilian workers.[16]

With more flight instructors and their families arriving daily, housing became an even more pressing problem. Two hundred civilian housing units were built by the government and all rents in town remained frozen. In a gracious gesture of civic generosity, M. L. Swineheart, the manager of the Pecos Chamber of Commerce, moved out of his own home so that the base commanding officer could have suitable housing.[17]

Lucy Kuykendall at last found a home of her own after months of living in a tiny tourist room at the Triangle Courts. All was not perfect in her new quarters, however. "Now I knew why the poets called it a little gray home in the West," she complained, "little because it was microscopic, and gray because it was covered with dust."[18]

Despite the personal hardships endured by nearly all newcomers, more arrived in Pecos daily. New cadet classes, averaging about 125 young men per class, arrived every four weeks. More cadets, of course, meant even more instructors who often brought their families with them. By 1943, the civilian population of the city itself was estimated to be just over 6,500, representing an increase of nearly 33 percent in three short years.[19]

The relationship between the longtime residents of Pecos and their newly acquired military neighbors was often less than harmonious. Lucy Kuykendall described the confrontation as "the battle of Pecos, a foolish bloodless feud."[20] The obvious cause of the feud was the great influx of army personnel into a community that was, as Kuykendall observed, "simply unprepared for such an explosive growth."[21]

There is much to indicate that the army was often impatient and heavy handed in dealing with the well-meaning but largely unsophisticated West Texans. When military inspectors found unsanitary conditions existing in many Pecos drugstores and cafes, the airfield's commander ordered the military police to guard the offending eating places to prohibit base personnel from entering. Mrs. Kuykendall wrote that the army also took it upon itself to improve the overall appearance of the town through the instigation of a rigorous clean-up campaign. "Tin cans, old iron beds, stoves, tires, disorderly stacks of lumber, and rusting pipes were to be seen in many yards," Kuykendall remembered, "but such eyesores soon disappeared under the Army's goading."[22]

Perhaps the one single event that the townspeople found most galling was the army's pronouncement that all milk obtained from Pecos area cows was heavily laced with bacteria carrying undulant fever, and clearly not fit for consumption by military personnel or, for that matter, anyone else. Milk for the airfield was then trucked in from Carlsbad, New Mexico, some eighty-five miles to the north. According to Mrs. Kuykendall, the citizens of Pecos "complained volubly, feeling that the Army's outlawing of their milk was a rank injustice."[23] Bill Pitts, who served as chairman of the 1998 reunion of Pecos veterans, had not been aware of the milk controversy when he served on the base late in the war. However, he had often wondered why he always saw hundreds of large milk cans in the cooling vault when he was on KP duty, and why there was no milk to be found in town.[24]

Kuykendall, being a native Texan as well as an officer's wife, heard all sides of the Pecos versus the army squabble. "The civilians told me," she wrote, "that the Army was an aggregation of hard-to-please snobs. Nothing seemed good enough for the snooty Army at [Pecos] field." Her friends in the army countered that the "civilians were a bunch of bloodsucking dumbclucks . . . getting rich off the Army." Perhaps deliberately overlooking Mrs. Kuykendall's Texas heritage, one officer's wife hurled her most damning adjectival epithet of all when she concluded, "The Pecos people are not only dumbclucks, they are Texas dumbclucks at that."[25] Kuykendall's response is not recorded.

Part of the social problems encountered during the airfield's early days seemed to stem from the office of the field commander, Col. H. C. Wisehart. The colonel, who had been at the base from its very first day, was a West Pointer and a stickler for proper military social decorum. To the people of Pecos, such traditional old army practices as leaving calling cards and serving high tea was alien, to say the very least. A strict disciplinarian and a firm believer in rigid adherence to military regulations, Wisehart asked more of both his command and his host city than either could possibly achieve. His replacement by Col. Orin J. Bushey in September 1943 was warmly welcomed by the soldiers and the townspeople alike.[26]

While the army and Pecos were having their cultural and social differences, the training regimen on the base continued at a brisk pace. In late 1943, it was announced that the mission of the base was to be changed from basic flight training to advanced multi-engine instruction. In time, Pecos was reputed to be the world's largest advanced flying school, and nearly 4,300 pilots graduated from the base's program.[27]

According to the men who trained there, life on Pecos Army Airfield was sharply focused on flying with little time for visits to the town or even pleasure jaunts to relatively nearby Mexico. Reminiscing at their reunion, the old flyers talked mainly of aircraft mechanical difficulties, the unreliability of navigational aids, and the day-to-day tedium of their eat-fly-sleep training schedule.

Most of the men claimed they only went into town once or twice during their entire nine-week stay at Pecos, but one long-time resident of the town, Bill Davenport, found reason to challenge that claim. Davenport served with the navy in the South Pacific during the war, and when he came back to his native Pecos at war's end, he found few eligible girls in town to date. "I guess the army boys liked our Texas gals," he remembered, "because when I got back here, almost all the good ones had married soldiers and moved away."[28]

Stan Brown, a soldier from California, recounted how disappointed his fiancée was when he decided they should postpone their wedding. After one look at the town, the base, and the ever present clouds of dust, Brown wired his intended bride that they would not be getting married until after his tour of duty in Pecos was completed. He explained that he could not bring her to live in a place where a glass of drinking water would have a thin film of mud on the top from the dust before he could sit down at a table to drink it.[29]

Of course, the army did bring some women of its own to Pecos. Two hundred Womens Army Corps (WAC) personnel and twenty-five Women Air Force Service Pilots (WASP) were stationed at the airfield. One veteran recalled that one of his friends lost his chance to become a pilot because of some confusion that occurred at the WAC barracks. Returning late to the field after perhaps consuming too many bottles of Lone Star beer at the Oasis Bar, the young pilot candidate had wandered into the WAC quarters, quite by accident, or so he insisted the next day. Accepting his claim that the incident was innocent and inadvertent, the authorities eliminated the officer from the flight training program nevertheless, citing his quite obvious lack of navigational aptitude.[30]

Other young pilot trainees apparently suffered from even more serious disorientation, but somehow survived to earn their wings. Several veterans related how they became lost while on night flights, and one reported landing on the south side of the Rio Grande when his aircraft was nearly out of fuel. The enterprising pilot bought some aviation gas from a Mexican airport employee and returned safely to Pecos. He thought it prudent not to relate his adventure to his superiors, and only when Mexican authorities belatedly reported the incident did he receive a severe reprimand for violating Mexican airspace.

Another young man made an emergency landing in a school

yard in New Mexico. His arrival created quite a stir among the local residents, and he enjoyed instant celebrity among the young women of the town who brought him food and drink to sustain him as he stayed with his plane overnight. About noon the next day, an army team came from Pecos to rescue him from what had developed into a pleasant, if unplanned, off-base adventure.[31]

L. R. McDonald, who was a flight supervisor during the war, remembered how one student pilot became completely lost on a solo cross-country flight. Finally spotting a town, the cadet flew low enough to see a sign reading "Crawford Hotel." As he had stayed at the Crawford in Carlsbad, New Mexico, just a few weeks earlier, he promptly landed his aircraft, pleased that he was not too far from his Pecos base. To his chagrin, he soon realized that he had in fact landed at Big Spring, Texas, well beyond the airfield's permissible cross-country flight zone. Only then did the young pilot learn that Big Spring had a Crawford Hotel of its own.[32]

When the hot West Texas skies became unbearable during training flights, some pilots found innovative ways to quench their thirst. Leslie Kleeb remembered that one of his instructors took over the controls of his aircraft and flew to Van Horn, Texas, where he adroitly landed it on the town's main street. The instructor then taxied the plane to a malt shop and told his cadet passenger to go inside and buy two malted milks. Once the refreshing drinks had been consumed, the pilot wheeled his aircraft back onto Main Street and took off to resume the in-flight training.[33]

Although their reminiscences are laden with tales of forced as well as intentional landings and of near misses in the air, it is clear that the men who trained at Pecos became highly qualified pilots. There can be no question that the flying regimen was not only demanding but often fatal. Many seasoned combat pilots who had initially relished their reassignment to Pecos as instructors soon requested a return to combat status in the theaters of war. Life as a flight instructor was to them demonstrably more hazardous than aerial combat had been.

THE AIR FORCE ERA AT PECOS COMES TO A CLOSE

By the spring of 1945, even though the war was still raging in the Pacific Theater, the Army Air Force determined that it had a more than adequate supply of pilots to fly its planes until the conflict could be successfully concluded. Consequently, the base was deactivated on April 30, and placed on a standby basis. Pecos Army Airfield remained inactive until just after V-J Day when dismantling operations began.

The Pecos Chamber of Commerce and City Council had made a valiant effort to convince the federal government that the facility could be put to some peacetime use, but to no avail. The wrecking crews fell upon the base's buildings with what must have been a great enthusiasm judging by the thoroughness of their handiwork.

Unlike many of the other towns being deprived of their military installations, however, Pecos had the foresight to request that some of the buildings be spared from razing and moved from the base into the city. As a result of that foresight, several of those buildings remain in use in Pecos today. Principal among the refurbished airfield buildings still in existence is the Pecos Fire Department headquarters located in the heart of the city. The entire huge brick edifice was transported the three mile distance from the base on a platform supported by seventy-two B-29 nose wheels. A church was also moved into town to be used by a local congregation, while what was once the Noncommissioned Officers Club (NCO) now houses both the Veterans of Foreign Wars and the American Legion Post, as well as a noisy cantina called *"El Suavecito."*

Where the mighty base once sprawled across the desert, there are but a few reminders of what had once dominated the landscape. The light tower with its rotating beacon remains, as does one runway that serves Pecos Municipal Airport. The NCO swimming pool is now a recreational facility, while what was the Officers Club pool is currently being used by members of the Pecos Valley Country Club. The swimming pool that was built solely for the use of the 290 black soldiers who were assigned to the base was filled with dirt after the war and used as part of the foundation for a home constructed for storied Texas wheeler-dealer, Billie Sol Estes. The house is now being used as a therapy center.[34]

A walk on what was once the bustling airfield yields little evidence to indicate that thousands of men and women once lived and worked here. Sidewalks lead to nothing and roads make their way to nowhere. Metal aircraft tie-down rings still gleam on the weed-covered asphalt ramps and aprons, and small piles of scrap metal are all that remain of a mess kitchen's cookstoves and a bakery's ovens. There is a hushed, almost haunted aura hovering over the entire massive site. It is exciting nonetheless to find a 1943 penny embedded in the asphalt of the crumbling taxiway, a coin perhaps dropped by a cadet hurrying to his BT-13, and to spot what is left of a rubber "Cat's Paw" heel, long separated from its government issue boot. Only the unmistakable and thrilling buzz of an angry snake's rattles can bring a halt to further exploration of the remains of a micro-civilization that once flourished in this forbidding desert land.

The reunited veterans seemed to have little if any interest in walking over their old training field. Of the 250 former cadets and instructors invited to attend the reunion, only twenty-five or so were willing or able to attend. By their own admission, their memories of life at Pecos are hazy now, over fifty years since they climbed into the cockpits of their UC72s or BT13s to soar into the bright blue West Texas sky. Maybe October was too hot for them to walk out on the runway that once welcomed them back to earth, or perhaps the dusty wind was just too strong. However, it could well be that they wanted to remember the vanished base the way it was long ago, lively and vital—just as they had been when they were boys of eighteen or nineteen.

The long suffering army wife, Lucy Kuykendall, seldom found much to remember fondly about Pecos, yet like most visitors to West Texas she was fascinated by its skies. "Who can forget the incredible Texas sky?" she once wrote, "How dwarfed I felt in its sudden vastness." When she saw her first sunset on the base, she was again moved to write, "At sunset, a flamingo radiance crept along the cool blue metal of the flight line, transforming the airplanes into a glittering collection of exotic fiery moths."[35]

All of those glittering airplanes are gone forever, eventually to be joined by the men who flew them. Only the rattlesnakes remain, once again sunning themselves on all that is left of Pecos Army Airfield.

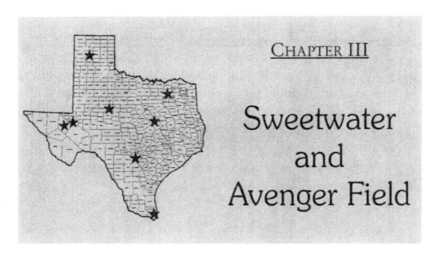

CHAPTER III

Sweetwater and Avenger Field

Well, I'm not near old enough to remember seeing any buffalo running around here, but my old granddaddy sure was and, boy, did he ever love to tell about seeing them. When those aeroplanes first started coming into Sweetwater over there, Granddad would just look up at them and shake his head. I guess he figured he'd seen about all there was to see by then.

Abel David Crane
Snyder, Texas
June 1998

Mr. Crane's grandfather and hundreds of his Sweetwater neighbors bore witness to both the final passing of the bison and the exciting advent of the airplane in a span of just thirty years. The community of Sweetwater served both as a supply center for buffalo hunters and, for a time, as a significant transportation hub in the newly born era of aviation.

Located some forty miles from the much larger city of Abilene, Sweetwater was named for the pleasantly potable water that once flowed in nearby Sweetwater Creek. A pioneering entrepreneur named Billie Knight had more or less established the settlement in 1877 when he opened a tent-housed store on the banks

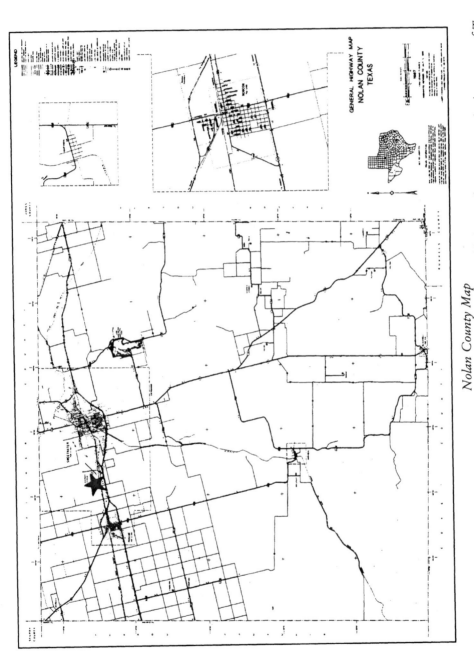

Nolan County Map

This map of North Central Nolan County shows the location of Avenger Field during the war years. An inset map of Texas shows the location of the county within the state.

of the creek, catering to the throngs of buffalo hunters who were annihilating the huge beasts that had long swarmed over the surrounding prairie.

Knight's store proved successful enough to spawn other business activities, and in 1879 a post office was opened. Three years later, the still tiny settlement of Sweetwater, consisting of little else but tents, dust, or mud, was named the seat of government for the newly formed Nolan County.

By 1883, spurred by the arrival of the Texas and Pacific Railroad, the population of the county continued to grow as did the number of saloons. Reflecting the influence of Sweetwater's saloons on the day-to-day life of the community, courthouse records show that an 1881-1883 grand jury handed down seventeen indictments for murder, another seventeen for assault to murder, and forty-five for gambling. The town's population was less than 1,000 at the time, and obviously was in some danger of shrinking even more.

By 1890, however, the census showed 1,573 people to be living in Sweetwater even though blizzards and drought had virtually destroyed the region's all-important agricultural activities only five years earlier. The arrival of the Kansas City, Mexico and Orient Railway in 1903 helped rescue the area from its weather-caused economic woes, and by 1930 Nolan County boasted a population of over 19,000. By 1940, Sweetwater itself had 10,367 residents with men working in the railroads' shops, at the International Harvester factory, or at the Gulf Oil Company's big refinery. The oil fields located throughout the county also offered good employment opportunities as did the large ranches that had somehow survived the Great Blizzard of 1885.

It was to be aviation, however, and not cattle, oil, or even railroads that would bring both excitement and economic growth to Sweetwater in the twentieth century. In 1911, just eight years after the Wright brothers' successful flight at Kittyhawk, North Carolina, one of the biplanes built by the famous brothers was flown to the community, landing in a field located near downtown.

The arrival of the Wright aeroplane by no means came as a surprise, as news of its anticipated coming had been heralded for weeks by Sweetwater's local newspapers. The plane's pilot, one Robert G. Fowler, was striving to collect a $50,000 prize being offered by publisher William Randolph Hearst to the first aviator to successfully complete a transcontinental flight across the United States. Arriving roughly on schedule at Sweetwater, Mr. Fowler was doubtless both impressed and amused to see from aloft that the well-meaning locals had spread a large bedsheet on the ground to serve as an aiming point for his landing. Successfully avoiding the sheet, Fowler managed to land his aircraft safely. Following an appropriately rowdy but seemingly heartfelt welcoming ceremony, he took to the air again in what ultimately proved to be a futile attempt to win Mr. Hearst's prize money. Although he did not prevail in the air race, Fowler did gain a somewhat less elevated place in local history as the first man ever to fly an airplane into Sweetwater, Texas.[1]

It was to be nearly ten years before the little town again experienced much in the way of aviation activity. Perhaps emboldened by the widely publicized daring feats of World War I aviators, a few local pilots acquired surplus army aircraft and began flying in and out of what had only recently been Sweetwater's rather rustic polo field located southwest of the town. Professional barnstormers also visited Sweetwater from time to time, luring air-minded and fearless citizens into their rickety biplanes for thrilling flights over the city. On one occasion, Sweetwater's old Wild West legacy got the better of contemporary modern technology when a herd of feral mules devoured much of the fabric covering the wings of an aircraft parked on a taxiway at the old polo field.[2]

Ravenous mules and direction indicators fashioned from bedsheets notwithstanding, Sweetwater managed to enjoy a growing reputation as a hospitable stopping point for aircraft flying west from Dallas to El Paso and back east again. In 1924, planes participating in the United States Army Air Service's first round-the-world flight touched down at the polo field-cum-landing strip, much to the delight of the local citizenry and particularly the school children who were excused from classes to witness the historic event. Many legendary figures of early aviation also landed at Sweetwater in the late 1920s and 1930s, including Jimmy Doolittle, Wiley Post, Claire L. Chennault, and the controversial prophet of air power, Gen. Billy Mitchell.[3]

The exciting comings and goings of such colorful pioneers of the air served to convince local civic leaders that aviation was destined to play a significant role in Sweetwater's future. It was also apparent that the old onetime polo ground was not going to be a suitable air facility for the illustrious future they so optimistically envisioned. By late summer 1929, the town's business and political leaders were successful in transforming Sweetwater's obvious affection for air travel into a tangible asset. The brand new Sweetwater Municipal Airport with its one hangar and its single oil-sprayed runway proudly opened for flight operations on August 10, 1929, the result of a highly successful community bond election campaign. Altruistic civic pride and fervent boosterism aside, however, well-conceived business interests had motivated the drive to place Sweetwater's name on the nation's rapidly developing aeronautical charts in a significant way. Soon, a clever plan to coordinate air and rail transportation was in operation, with travelers being able to fly to Sweetwater from St. Louis on Safeway Airline's Ford Tri-motors and then board the Texas and Pacific Railway's coaches bound for Los Angeles. Return trips were also available. The scheme was an instant success and Sweetwater seemed poised to become a major hub for transcontinental travel.[4]

As exciting and impressive as the town's growth had been as an air and rail terminus, the situation changed abruptly when the Great Depression finally made its way westward and into Texas in 1930. The air-rail connection was soon discontinued and what had been a growing air freight business ended almost overnight as interstate commerce activity plummeted. With the entire country in economic turmoil, Sweetwater Municipal Airport, even with its then state of the art beacons and other night flying aids, remained for the most part idle and all but deserted. Only a New Deal Works Project Administration (WPA) construction project kept the once proud airport from slipping into total decay, but the tight grip of economic stagnation with no sign of relief portended a bleak future for Sweetwater's once soaring dreams of being a major air transportation hub.

As was the case all across America, however, it took a war, or at least the prospect of one, to break the stranglehold of the depression. Long before it officially entered World War II, the United States began to prepare for a major war that seemed all but certain to come. CAA airport survey teams, seeking possible sites for the training bases that would be needed if and when war finally came, visited Sweetwater on several occasions late in 1939. While taking note of the clear skies and the virtual absence of rain or any other form of precipitation, the site teams were particularly impressed by the existing runway, the excellent railway and highway accessibility, and the navigational and night flying aids already in place but for the most part being used only rarely.

Needless to say, the leaders of the economically distressed community were overjoyed to learn from representatives of the federal government that Sweetwater Municipal Airport was being seriously considered as a possible army airfield. Fully a year before Pearl Harbor and America's entry into the war in December 1941, the town's city commissioners voted overwhelmingly to take whatever steps were necessary to ensure that the United States government would decide favorably to establish a training facility at the town's municipal airport.

With remarkable unanimity, the city fathers promptly set about acquiring more land adjacent to the existing airport, and soon received a commitment from the federal government for $190,000 in funds to supplement the local expenditures. Although the expansion of the airport facility was ostensibly to be strictly a civil endeavor, there was little if any doubt that the field was in fact being hurriedly readied for military use when the need arose.

By January 1941, all of the required land had been purchased at a figure of less than $100 per acre. Later that same year, the planned initial improvements and expansion work on the thirteen-year-old, six-hundred-acre field were complete. Just one week into that final month of 1941, the Japanese attack on Pearl Harbor finally brought the United States into a world war. Like many other quickly but quietly expanded air facilities across Texas, Sweetwater Municipal Airport had in fact been ready to go to war months before the conflict actually started.

The good people of Sweetwater, passionately patriotic and eager to help win that war in any way they possibly could, were in for a few surprises, particularly if they expected only poster-perfect young American men to be serving at the new airfield. The first surprise came when the first fledgling pilots to come to Sweetwater Municipal were not Americans at all, but young British men being trained to fly with the Eagle Squadron of the Royal Air Force. The Plosser and Prince Air Academy had gained a contract through President Franklin D. Roosevelt's Lend-Lease program to train the

Britishers, teaching them to fly at various U.S. Army airfields. The firm's principals found Sweetwater to be an excellent location for the English cadets, and the city of Sweetwater obligingly leased the newly expanded airport to Plosser and Prince for one dollar per year for a ten-year period starting on April 1, 1942.[5]

The contractors promptly invested an additional $100,000 in further expansion on the base to prepare it for the incoming class of foreign aviation cadets. New hangars, dining facilities, and dormitories were soon under construction. The city's municipal airport, almost overnight, had grown to be a major military air facility and the people of Sweetwater felt a swelling pride in their town's war effort as well as a growing satisfaction in its improving economy. From a tiny airport valued at $15,000 in 1929, the expanded facility was now worth well over $2 million.[6]

Somehow, though, the name "Sweetwater Municipal" just did not seem to have a very warlike ring to it. Patriotically putting pride in their city's name aside for the duration, community leaders were soon seeking a more bellicose sounding title to appropriately reflect the facility's new military mission. The local newspaper ran a contest offering a fifty dollar war bond to the creative local individual who suggested the best new name for the base. The winner was Mrs. Grace Favor, who put her thoughts more or less into rhyme. In her final stanza, Mrs. Favor penned:

> *Sleep on martyr'd dead, you have*
> *not died in vain!*
> *The torch we'll bear . . . nor to the*
> *despot yield*
> *'Til all is safe for peace throughout*
> *the world.*
> *Your purpose shall be served,*
> *Avenger Field!*[7]

Thus, in an emotional tribute to those who had lost their lives at Pearl Harbor, Sweetwater Field became Avenger Field, at least for the duration of the war. The airport's name was officially changed to Avenger Field on May 14, 1942, and Mrs. Favor was given her bond.[8]

By the end of the month of its re-christening, the first of the

British cadets began arriving at the newly named field. For the fifty young Englishmen, West Texas was a "terribly, terribly strange place," as one cadet from Lancashire put it. "There was not a blade of grass to be seen and the people seemed to be universally huge. I felt like a dwarf in the desert the whole time I was there."[9]

To their credit, the permanent residents, however gigantic they may have appeared to foreign eyes, accepted their visitors good-naturedly. Although the English accents of the cadets caused many embarrassing misunderstandings, the Britishers and the Texans got on surprisingly well with each other. One now-retired rancher who was in high school when the cadets first came to town recalled that although in his later years he had traveled extensively in Germany, Japan, and France, the language barrier between the Texans and the British somehow seemed the most formidable he had ever encountered. "I never misunderstood any language anywhere else in the world as much as I did the English jargon those young fly-boys talked," he remembered, "but we all had a lot of fun trying to figure out what we thought we heard them say."[10]

By all accounts, the experience was rewarding for the visitors as well as for the hosts. When they were not flying, the cadets visited ranches, saw rodeos, ate barbecue for the first time in their lives, and attended church services as the Anglican guests of lifelong Baptists and Methodists. At the annual Fourth of July extravaganza in Sweetwater in 1942, ironically celebrating as it did America's independence from England, the cadets surprised the home crowd of Texans by singing several choruses of "Deep in The Heart of Texas." The memory of that spontaneous serenade is still fresh in the minds of the few remaining old-time residents who heard it sung that hot night so long ago.[11]

It was with genuine regret that the city received the news that the British training program at Avenger Field was to end with the graduation of the first fifty-cadet class in August 1942. However, when it was promptly announced that at long last American aviation cadets would soon be arriving at the field, the citizens of Sweetwater were ecstatic, particularly those young girls who entertained thoughts of perhaps acquiring a dashing young officer-to-be as a husband. Emily Turner Cole, only eighteen when the first U.S. Army aviation cadets arrived in Sweetwater, recalled the impression the newly arrived young men had made upon her. "Oh, they were just beautiful. That's the only word for it. They were just plain beautiful," she remembered fondly. "They were all tall, or so it seems to me now, and all of them were so handsome and so proud. I don't think the boys in our school were too happy to have them camped out there west of town, but we girls were just thrilled about the whole idea of it."[12]

Less than a month after the American aviation cadet program had replaced the British training scheme, an additional instructional curriculum was introduced at Avenger Field on an experimental basis. Under what was known as the Air Transport Command Training Program, selected enlisted and civil service personnel possessing satisfactory levels of flight instruction were scheduled to undergo an accelerated course in multi-engine training. It was hoped that after successfully completing the additional fifty hours of in-flight instruction, the new pilots would be qualified to fly the army's larger transport aircraft. This newly created manpower pool, it was reasoned, would free other commissioned pilots to fly bombers and fighters in the combat zones.

Although the original course planning called for 150 students to participate in the program, the school's officials were chagrined when only one enlisted man was found to be adequately qualified to enter the first class in September 1942. Over the next few months, an additional sixty-eight candidates were accepted into the program, but after over half of those were duly eliminated, the experiment was abruptly canceled.[13]

Under the ongoing training program, however, 820 aviation cadets received their flight instruction at Avenger Field from August 1942 through early April 1943. Perhaps fortunately for the town, but understandably frustrating to the cadets, discipline was rigid and frequent access to Sweetwater and to the idolizing young female population was highly restricted. However, there is much evidence that many starry-eyed damsels continued to dream of stalwart young airmen and not always in vain. In the spring of 1943, however, any dreams of a long or even short-term relationship with the all-American male cadets came abruptly to an end.

THE WOMEN AIRFORCE SERVICE PILOTS (WASP)
ARRIVE AT SWEETWATER

*Right after Pearl Harbor happened, a lot of the boys from
around Sweetwater left home to go into the service and
our airport was turned into a big Army airfield. Then, all
of a sudden, we read in the paper that all of those nice
young men out there were going to be sent off somewhere
to make room for a bunch of women pilots who were on
their way. Well, I'll tell you that when I heard about
women pilots being in Sweetwater, I thought, what is this
world coming to?*

> Millicent Bond McKee
> Abilene, Texas
> June 1998

In July 1942, the Army Air Force's chief, Gen. Henry H.
Arnold, issued a statement that, "The use of women pilots serves no
military purpose."[14] By early the next year, however, facing an
alarming shortage of pilots of any gender, the general had completely changed his mind about the need to use women in military
flying capacities excluding only actual combat situations. Urged to
do so by famed aviatrix, Jacqueline Cochran, Arnold created the
WASP. Although originally headquartered in Houston, it would be
at Sweetwater's Avenger Field where over one thousand WASP
earned their wings. From the West Texas field, the women pilots
went on to perform highly commendable and often heroic, but for
the most part officially unrecognized, service to their country.

Shortly after the women's program moved to Avenger in 1943,
the field became the only all-female training base in the United
States. When the WASP first arrived at Sweetwater, however, there
was a brief period when the last class of male cadets was still on the
base and occupying some of the barracks. Although the newly
arrived female trainees were at least theoretically isolated in what
many of them considered to be far too much of a convent-like existence, cadets of both sexes soon found ways to socialize even after
Taps had sounded across the West Texas prairies.

The first Sweetwater class of the WASP arrived at Avenger

Field in March 1943 and was designated 43-W-5. The "W" in the official class designation not very subtly identified the group as being made up solely of women. While the program had originated in Houston in January 1943, the Army Air Force, attracted by the wide open spaces of West Texas and the welcome absence of any traditional big city distractions, decided to move the training program some four hundred miles northwest to Sweetwater. As the class flew toward its new base, it stopped for a lunch break in San Angelo. In the air base cafeteria there, the thirty-nine young women lunched by themselves in a corner, finding amusement in whistling at any good looking army man who captured their collective fancy. Was small-town Sweetwater in any way prepared to accept such unheard of behavior by its new female guests?

The official history of Nolan County indeed notes with perhaps some degree of wry understatement that "the advent of the girls to Avenger Field was received with mixed emotions by the citizens and field personnel alike."[15] One authority of the WASP was a bit more direct in her assessment of Sweetwater's reception of the idea of an all-girl base. "Now the town swarmed with pretty, self-assured girls on Saturday night, not handsome young fellows," noted the writer, "and Sweetwater families with marriageable daughters weren't happy about the situation."[16] Seemingly Sweetwater's principal social problem, at least initially, was not the arrival of the young women at Avenger Field but the departure of the young men from it.

The pretty and allegedly self-assured girls themselves were by no means universally overjoyed at the prospect of spending the next six months of their lives in what most of them perceived to be a remote and desolate corner of the world. One observer of the WASP experience points out that, "Sweetwater at that time [1943] resembled the standard movie depiction of a small Texas cowboy town." There were big hats, boots and spurs, "and even a few guns were visible." According to this same source, these colorful and rough characters "presented an impressive sight to the incoming WASP, many of whom arrived from eastern cities."[17]

An editorial in an early edition of the official WASP newspaper, *The Avenger*, indicates that the West Texas town did not readily embrace the newcomers. As the editor saw it:

> They [the townspeople] didn't understand us and so misjudged
> us. In the first place, we came here with two strikes against us. We
> were women pilots—a profession which, until recently has carried
> the stigma attached to the girls who rode "astride" in the days of
> the side-saddle skirt. We are supposed to be rough and uncouth
> and not quite right in the head.

In closing her article, the editor let slip that perhaps some of the
misunderstanding and misjudgment might well have been deserved.
"When a few of us let down our hair and broke the tension," she
lamented, "we acquired the titles of 'drunks and roughnecks,' an
unfair and not very far-seeing conclusion."[18]

To arrive in Sweetwater to this less than open-armed reception,
the candidates for WASP training had to provide their own transportation. Further, to qualify for admission into the program, each
woman was required to be a licensed pilot and to have logged thirty-
five hours of flying time. As the cost of acquiring a private pilot's
license in the early 1940s was approximately $700, the 25,000 ap-
plicants for WASP training represented an elevated segment of
American womanhood, figuratively as well as literally.[19]

Included in the group of successful candidates over the two-
year life of the WASP program were a professional golfer, an heiress
to the Florsheim shoe fortune, a daughter of Oklahoma's oil-rich
Kerr family, and the world's first woman commercial pilot. Also
accepted into the program over the years were a ski-team manager,
several models, a biologist, a housewife and mother of three, as well
as the only female co-pilot then flying for the Peruvian national airline. One candidate, Helen Richey, had once been Amelia Earhart's
co-pilot, while Mary Wiggins had been a Hollywood stunt flyer
before volunteering for WASP training. The wife of popular writer
Damon Runyan also came to Sweetwater as did the experienced
pilot Irene I. Crum, who had already logged over 3,000 hours of flying time prior to her arrival at Avenger Field.[20]

The 1,830 successful candidates selected from the 25,000 original applicants arrived by train and by automobile and several flew
to Texas in their own airplanes. Their pay was little and their
benefits all but non-existent. The WASP who earned their wings at
Avenger Field and went on to fly on active duty as civil service
pilots were denied such standard government-provided amenities as

insurance, uniform allowances, pensions, or even a cost-free funeral in the event of their death while on active service. Thirty-eight of the women did die in service related accidents, and they were each buried at their own family's personal expense. The only substantive rewards for the WASP were the opportunity to serve their country in wartime, and to fly any and all of the aircraft that a reluctant army would permit them to take aloft.

Even the most patriotic, selfless, and eager to fly WASP candidate must have had second thoughts upon arriving at Avenger Field. One writer describes the weather conditions in West Texas with great accuracy when she notes that, "The temperature often reached 100° in April and stayed there for five months."[21] The wind was, and still is, noted for blowing at least twenty-five miles per hour each and every day most times of the year. In her master's thesis written in 1934, Louise Bradford, a native of Sweetwater, made firsthand reference to the constant West Texas breezes. "The most characteristic feature of the climate is the wind . . . characterized by its intense heat and extreme dryness." If the heat and dryness were not dubious qualities enough, Ms. Bradford also commented on the sand which, "was the weapon of the wind; it stung the face like bits of glass; it blinded the eyes."[22] Nine years after Bradford's paper was submitted to the University of Texas, the newcomers to Avenger Field could have easily endorsed as valid her observations about the wind and sand. Indeed, the motto of the WASP was, "We live in the wind and the sand . . . and our eyes are on the stars."[23]

With all of its fabled harshness of weather, however, there was one thing about West Texas that enamored it to all aviators, female and male alike. Charlotte Mitchell of the Class of 43-W-5 remembered watching her first Texas sunset with her baymates from the window of their barracks. As the sky turned "from rose to orange to crimson," Charlotte and her fellow WASP suddenly realized that "they were in Texas because of its wide, spectacular sky."[24]

Spectacular though it was, the Texas sky also proved to be a tough training classroom for the WASP candidates. The contract flight instructors were firm and thorough in teaching the young women the army way of flying just as they had previously been when instructing the young men, and to the great surprise of some, the women learned their lessons well. Statistics would soon show that the washout rate for the women pilots-to-be was actually less than that for male aviation cadets. Over the two-year period of the WASP training program, only 30 percent of the candidates failed to receive their wings. In comparison, a four-year period of flight instruction for male pilot candidates yielded a 40 percent rate of failure. Further, the WASP accident rate per flying hour was lower than that of their male counterparts. It in no way detracts from the WASP overall flying abilities to note that these statistics compare the performance records of the already licensed and at least some-what experienced women pilots with male trainees who were for the most part novices just learning to fly.[25]

The training records attained by the WASP did not come easily. Clad in their ill-fitting flight coveralls dubbed "zoot suits" that were issued in men's size 44 only, the young women rapidly made the transition from the low horsepower aircraft in which they had initially learned to fly to the much more powerful PT-19 trainers. When they were not in the air learning to master the bigger planes, the women were enduring the army's seemingly sadistic penchant for calisthenics. When performed in the blazing Texas sun, the exercises proved to be particularly fatiguing and irritating, but most of the candidates persevered. Many steaming hours in cramped Link Trainers also proved to be highly uncomfortable, but invaluable in mastering the more advanced aircraft.

After hours of intensive ground instruction and two weeks of flying training, the pilots were ready to attempt a solo flight in the PT-19s. After successfully completing the solo flight and surviving the traditional dunking by their compatriots in the WASP wishing well, each pilot next flew to the assigned aerial training areas near the field to practice on a daily basis. They were also required to take cross-country flights to any domestic destination of their choice. Surviving journals and diaries indicate that many of the women pilots made the most of this official opportunity to enjoy a brief respite from Avenger Field's severely restricted social life.

The West Texas sky was literally teeming with pilot trainees in 1943, each eager to earn the aviator's coveted wings. When the word spread with unsurprising rapidity that Avenger Field had become an all-female base, interest in visiting the Sweetwater facility suddenly surged among the many male cadets based within flying distance. Unfortunately for the ardent young men, the only acceptable excuse for landing at Avenger was a declared in-flight emergency.

Within one short week, over one hundred such so-called emergencies compelled male cadets to touch down at the Sweetwater field. When it soon became apparent that the only verifiable urgency that had brought about the emergency landings was the understandable desire of the lonely male cadets to visit the glamorous lady pilots, Avenger's commanding officer closed the field to all but his own training aircraft.[26]

One WASP candidate, however, inadvertently made it unnecessary for one group of fortunate male cadets to touch down at Sweetwater to catch a fleeting glimpse of a female flyer. Caught up in the exhilaration of solo flight, the WASP removed her shirt to soak up the sun's rays in the open cockpit of her PT-19 trainer. To her mortification, she suddenly found herself in the midst of a formation made up of several aircraft from a nearby base, each piloted by a gaping and admiring young male cadet. As she ducked out of sight in an effort to get back into a more decorous uniform, she accidentally let the shirt slip from her grasp, and watched red-faced as it took flight out of the cockpit and off into space. Having provided much more exposure than she had ever intended, she flew hurriedly back to Avenger still accompanied by her gleeful multi-plane and all-male escort formation.[27]

Despite such rare mishaps, however, the training regimen was serious and stringent. Discipline was strict and only rarely did the young women get passes to go into town to meet their civilian neighbors. Although the citizens of Sweetwater were slow to accept these pants-wearing women who smoked, sunbathed, and dared to fly airplanes, the WASP eventually came to be accepted, at least for the most part. Wetsel's Beauty Shop announced in a late 1943 newspaper advertisement that the shop was to be reserved each Saturday afternoon for the exclusive use of the WASP. In the summer, the women were invited to use the municipal swimming pool, but strict measures were taken to ensure that they did not mingle with local swimmers. The pool was reserved for the WASP for two hours every Monday, Wednesday, and Friday.[28]

Some of the young flyers attended church services in town and occasionally they were invited to have Sunday dinner at the homes of the regular parishioners. On rare occasions, unfortunately, the invitations proved to be less than heartfelt and the visitors found themselves being asked to eat in the kitchen while the family ate in the dining room. Other families grew close to the lonely young women, however, and several virtually adopted whole groups of WASP, sharing their hopes and sorrows and making them a part of a newly extended Texas family.

Through the public relations efforts of Jacqueline Cochran, the WASP indefatigable founder and champion, Sweetwater eventually began to open its doors more widely and more sincerely to the young pilots. In time, the townspeople even sponsored a service club for the women to use when they came to town. Called the Avengerette Club, the facility provided a place to listen to music and drink Coca-Cola until curfew time sent them scurrying back to the field on the base bus. Although Sweetwater and all of Nolan County still legally prohibited the sale of alcoholic beverages, some worldly women of the WASP soon located an elderly gray-haired gift shop owner who thought it her patriotic duty to sell bottles of what was described as being "fairly good bourbon" for two dollars a pint. A quick visit to this grandmotherly bootlegger's shop before going on to the Avengerette Club ensured that the Coca-Colas had an appreciably stronger bite to them.[29]

On one occasion, a wayward WASP forgot about one of Sweetwater's rather restrictive Blue Laws and committed the locally unpardonable sin of sitting on a park bench after 9:00 P.M. Whether or not under the influence of Granny's bootleg liquor, the young woman was promptly thrown into the city jail. Quickly regaining her freedom, she nevertheless received ten demerits for being ten minutes late in returning to the airfield. For a woman, WASP or otherwise, sitting on a Sweetwater park bench as late as 9:01 at night in 1943 was clearly a costly offense.[30]

Despite, or perhaps because of, such daring misadventures, the WASP became virtual idols to many teenage girls living in Nolan County at the time. Watching from a respectful distance as the tanned and physically fit young flyers smoked and laughed at Sweetwater's municipal pool, one sixteen-year-old Texas girl realized that it was possible for women to be more than wives of cowboys or oil field workers. "I'll never forget them," she wrote. "They were so independent and so self-assured. To me, they symbolized what I had suspected for some time, there truly could be a bright future for us girls beyond the city limits of Sweetwater if we wanted to seek it."[31]

For the most part, WASPs with rare weekend passes to leave

the airfield tended to stay together as a group either on visits to Sweetwater or nearby Abilene. There were very few eligible civilian males around and fraternization with the civilian instructors from the base or with any army personnel was officially forbidden. Although off-duty liaisons with the instructors were specifically against regulations, several of the graduates eventually married the men who had helped them earn their wings at Avenger Field.

During the nearly two years that the WASP program was at Avenger, 1,074 candidates successfully completed the training and received their wings. Apparently, the actual pinning of the silver wings on the uniforms of the successful graduates presented considerable problems on occasion to the male officers in charge of the awarding ceremonies. One colonel urgently whispered to the first WASP he intended to present with her wings that, "I've done this for hundreds of cadets, but I've never pinned wings on a woman before. If I stick you, for heaven's sake don't jump. My wife is in the first row and I'd never live it down."[32]

Even the indomitable Hap Arnold had difficulty in affixing wings or medals on the service jackets of the WASP. The general, who had very frequently presented such awards to his fellow male aviators, always made it a practice to unbutton the top of the jacket so that he might slip his hand inside it to secure the pins holding the award in place. It was reported that when Arnold had his first occasion to decorate the uniform jacket of a WASP with a medal, he unthinkingly resorted to his customary manner of presentation. When it suddenly occurred to him what he was about to do, an observer reported that, "It was a toss-up as to whose face was redder, the commanding general's or that of the blushing WASP."[33] Thereafter, following this memorable incident, Arnold usually preferred to hand the silver wings to the young women so that they might pin them on for themselves.

By early 1944, it had become apparent to General Arnold that the WASP program was an unqualified success. "I am looking forward to the day," said the proud general, "when Womens Airforce Service Pilots take the place of practically all AAF pilots in the United States for the duration."[34]

Once they had graduated, the WASP did indeed serve with distinction throughout the war. They had gone on active duty in a variety of flying assignments that released male pilots for combat duty.

Restricted from actual combat themselves, the women towed gunnery targets, performed dangerous test pilot duties, and ferried aircraft to the very periphery of the actual combat zones. In total, the women pilots eventually logged over sixty million air miles in the course of the war. Experiencing a low fatality rate per hours flown despite the great risks involved, the WASP piloted virtually every aircraft in the Army Air Force's arsenal, including P-51s, B-17s, and B-29s.[35]

When male pilots were initially hesitant to fly the new but bulky B-29 because of its size, a twenty-five-year-old lieutenant colonel named Paul Tibbetts asked WASPs Dora Dougherty and Dorothea Johnson to take one of the huge aircraft on a series of demonstration flights over New Mexico carrying as passengers the male pilots who had expressed doubts about the aircraft's reliability. Though Tibbetts's use of the female aviators to embarrass the regular male flight crews into accepting the big plane was successful, it was not appreciated by the air force's high command in Washington, and the WASP were promptly restricted from flying the B-29s that Tibbetts would eventually make famous in his historic mission over Hiroshima on August 6, 1945.[36]

Seeking a way to suitably reward his heroic women pilots for their commendable service, General Arnold made a valiant and sincere effort to have them commissioned as army officers. While generally recognizing the praiseworthy services of the WASP, the U.S. Congress refused Arnold's request. Further, the Congress soon came to the conclusion that there were now enough male pilots available to handle both combat and non-combat flying duties.

When it soon appeared that the congressionally declared surplus of male pilots might result in the outright termination of the WASP program, the citizens of Sweetwater rallied behind an all-out effort to keep open the women pilot training facility that had once been so locally controversial. A front page story in *The Avenger* of July 14, 1944, stated that, "Congressmen, senators, and women's organizations throughout the United States have been contacted by Sweetwater citizens and asked to aid in saving the WASP program."[37] All of their determined efforts were in vain, however, and the air force was compelled to terminate the program by the end of 1944. Gen. Henry H. Arnold himself addressed the final graduating class of the WASP in December 1944. With tears glistening on their cheeks, the graduates proudly sang the lyrics that their fellow graduates had sung throughout the years the WASP had been at Avenger Field, to the tune of "Yankee Doodle Dandy."

> *We are the Yankee Doodle pilots,*
> *Yankee Doodle do or die.*
> *Real live nieces of our Uncle Sam,*
> *born with a yearning to fly.*
> *Keep in step to all our classes,*
> *march to flight line with our pals.*
> *Yankee Doodle came to Texas*
> *just to fly the "PTs."*
> *We are those Yankee Doodle gals!*[38]

One teary-eyed observer noted that even the usually smiling but nonetheless crusty Gen. Hap Arnold suddenly found it necessary to look away for a moment during the highly emotional ceremonies, away into that spectacular Texas sky that had brought them all together at Sweetwater.[39]

Although the WASP were promptly disbanded and gone from Avenger Field, there was still a war going on elsewhere in the world. Soon, the base which had been virtually undergoing continuous expansion since its inception in 1940, was found to be a suitable site for an advanced fighter pilot training base. Consequently, on January 24, 1945, the first contingent of fighter pilots arrived by train in Sweetwater to a tumultuous welcome by the local citizenry. Simultaneously, a flight of the field's new operational aircraft, the Republic P-47 Thunderbolt, roared over the large welcoming crowd, causing babies to cry, dogs to bark, and, once again, young girls' hearts to beat perhaps a little faster.

Even though the Axis powers were clearly in disarray and victory was now generally assumed to be close at hand, extensive new construction continued on the base and flight training was scheduled at an almost hectic pace. At the time of Japan's formal surrender and the official end of the war in September 1945, nearly 150 commissioned air officers were still undergoing advanced fighter training at Avenger Field.[40]

Suddenly, however, it was all over except for the celebratory parades and the homecoming speeches. Inactivity soon replaced frantic construction at Avenger Field, and the howling of the West Texas wind replaced the roar of the Thunderbolts. Declared surplus by the federal government, the once vital facility simply ceased to have a life. Its many wartime missions successfully accomplished, Avenger Field was apparently destined to quietly surrender itself back to the harsh prairie from which it had risen only a half-decade earlier.

ANOTHER WAR BRINGS PLANES BACK TO AVENGER FIELD

It was kind of sad to see it all go back to dust. For a time during the war, that airfield out there was just about the most exciting place around. Pretty soon though, they opened her back up and things started buzzing again.

E. Robert Pearsall
Abilene, Texas
June 1998

It took the federal government nearly two years to officially close Avenger Field and return the facility to the city of Sweetwater. On June 3, 1947, however, the four hangars, the administration building, the control tower, and seventeen other structures were classified as surplus and conveyed back to the city government that had so eagerly struggled to create the base not ten years before.

Following a period of sporadic civilian flight activity, Avenger Field again returned to military status in April 1952 following the beginning of the Korean War. The U.S. Defense Department leased a portion of the field for use as an auxiliary landing facility for pilots in training at nearby Webb Air Force Base at Big Spring. Once again, more federal money was appropriated to further improve Avenger's runways, and the jet trainers of the U.S. Air Force soon screamed over Sweetwater.

While the practice landings and take-offs continued, the Defense Department also commenced construction on a major radar installation at the base. Designed to be part of a national early warning system to detect possible Soviet incursions into continental air space, the so-called Site M-89 was manned by an aircraft control and warning squadron of the air force. By June 1956, the radar warning site was in full operation as part of the national surveillance network, with 198 men being listed on the squadron's rolls.

The radar defense system remained active through 1969, and Avenger Field continued to benefit from sizable federal investments in improvements and construction projects. A housing complex was built, the base's streets were re-paved, and both NCO and officers' clubs were re-established. A new dining hall was built, along with a large multi-use recreation building. The city, delighted to have a military neighbor once again, donated a rest and recreation facility at nearby Lake Sweetwater to the base.

Despite the large amounts of local and federal funds that had been expended at Avenger since World War II, the base was again marked for closure in September 1969. The financial loss to the Sweetwater economy was conservatively projected to be over $1 million per year. Fortunately for the city, however, a plan for utilizing newly closed air force bases as educational facilities had proved to be successful at Waco, Harlingen, and Amarillo. Under the plan, the Texas State Technical Institute, now known as Texas State Technical College (TSTC), transformed the military sites into technical training institutions, using the recently vacated buildings as classrooms, shops, dormitories, and libraries. After considerable political maneuvering at the state capital, the school managed to convene its first classes at Avenger Field in September 1970. In time, the school proved to be a success and a fitting capstone to Sweetwater's dedication to its airfield. Unlike other once vital air facilities that have faded into non-existence, Avenger Field lives on into the twenty-first century.

While little remains of the World War II buildings on the old base, there is historic evidence of the increasingly fabled presence of the WASP. Their wishing well is still in place, now framed by two long walls of Texas granite inscribed with the names of the women who learned to fly the army way at Avenger Field. Gold stars mark the names of those who died while doing so. A statue of a WASP has been erected and a state historical marker tells the story of Avenger Field and the remarkable women who made it famous.

From time to time, the last of the surviving WASP come back

to Avenger Field. At their fiftieth reunion in 1993, 250 of the one-time highly skilled pilots marched proudly through the streets of Sweetwater, many of them still trim enough to wear the uniforms of Santiago blue issued to them a half-century before. The adoring little town loved them all. Ann Richards, then the governor of the state, welcomed them back to Texas and a sleek B-1B bomber from Abilene's Dyess Air Force Base screamed past in a fitting low-level salute to the dwindling number of heroic women pilots who had defied convention, overcome social censure, and had earlier dared to fly other big planes in the dark days of World War II.[41]

For a brief moment, the once bustling field echoed again with the chatter and laughter of the storied veterans, still for the most part as self-assured and independent as ever. After the luncheon and the speeches, and after the final farewells, the WASP left Avenger Field, some of them perhaps forever. Following the heartfelt reception they had just received, perhaps their lasting memories of Sweetwater, Texas, would always be fond ones.

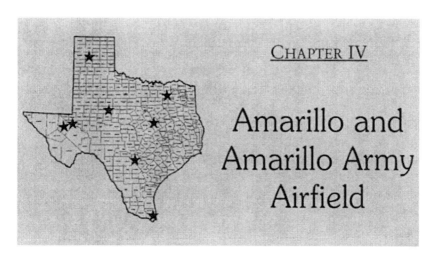

CHAPTER IV

Amarillo and Amarillo Army Airfield

It was both the hottest and the coldest place I was ever stationed at. And then there was that damn wind blowin' day and night, but you know something? I always liked it up there in the Panhandle, but don't ask me why.

George F. (Bud) Belcher
Fort Worth, Texas
October 1998

Even the earliest visitors to the sprawling Texas Panhandle often found it necessary to comment on the region's capricious and often extreme weather conditions. When the legendary Spanish *conquistador* Francisco de Coronado led his helmeted legions across the trackless Panhandle landscape in 1541, one of his lieutenants kept a journal of daily events and climatic changes. What struck him even more forcefully than the area's red soil and deep canyons was the suddenness with which a balmy late spring day could be instantly transformed into a wintry nightmare, with blizzards of snow and sleet becoming equally paralyzing blizzards of dirt and sand in a matter of mere minutes.[1]

Long after the Spanish adventurers had experienced the dreaded Texas blue northers, early-day United States Army explorers concluded that the unpredictable weather and often unforgiving

51

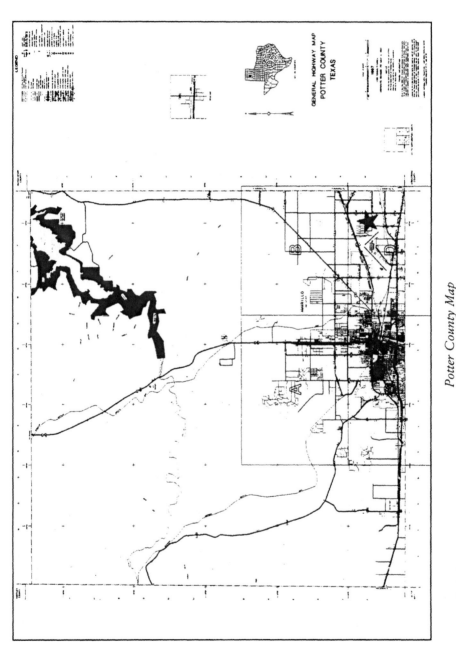

Potter County Map

This map of southern Potter County shows the location of Amarillo Army Airfield during the war years. An inset map of Texas shows the location of the county within the state.

terrain of the region would cause it to be forever known as the Great American Desert. Late in the nineteenth century, however, at the very center of that inhospitable desert, the city of Amarillo, Texas, came into being. Although other tentative communities had earlier struggled to survive in the Panhandle, first as supply depots for buffalo hunters and then as lawless rest and recreation centers for the area's exuberant cowhands, the coming of the railroad to Amarillo in 1887 virtually ensured the tiny community's future as the principal city of the entire region.

In early 1887, real estate speculator J. T. Berry had platted and begun development of the fledgling Amarillo well in advance of the widely publicized future route of the railroad. Selling lots in his new development for up to $100 each, Berry promptly established a post office, a newspaper, and a fairly reputable small hotel as if to reassure his investors that they had indeed made a wise financial decision, while hopefully convincing others to do the same. Originally given the name Oneida by its developer, the little town soon became more popularly known as Amarillo. The new name purportedly stemmed from a Spanish word meaning yellow, and was chosen because of the seasonal color of the all too few lakes and streams to be found in the vicinity. The name change was apparently popular with most of the town's residents who promptly painted the sides of their houses a bright yellow color by way of appropriate celebration.[2]

Two of Berry's rivals, Henry B. Sanborn and Joseph Glidden, were by no means convinced that the brightly painted new town had much of a future, however, quickly pointing out that the little community was in imminent danger of being flooded. As a hedge against this dire possibility, the two developers had prudently acquired some 2,560 acres of apparently floodproof land immediately adjacent to the imperiled town. The men then graciously offered to move the few existing buildings from the possibly endangered Amarillo onto their land in order to create a new city that would be safe from any flooding that might possibly occur, even though contemporary records clearly indicated that fewer than ten inches of rain were likely to fall in any given year. Several of the more easily persuaded townsfolk accepted the offer made by Sanborn and Glidden, and permitted their homes to be moved to the newer and ostensibly safer community located just east of their original homesites. To convince others to move to the new town, the two developers donated land for a church and even built a rather elegant hotel.

In the spring of 1889, just two years after its founding, the original Amarillo was indeed completely inundated as predicted when a freak thunderstorm dropped more than an average year's worth of rain on the unfortunate little village in just one day's time. Ironically, a track embankment built by the very railroad that had first brought life to the now swamped Amarillo had acted as a dam during the deluge, impounding the yellow waters of the rain-swollen creeks and destroying the town.[3]

All of those who managed to survive the great flood hastily moved to the newer, safer, and much dryer Amarillo that had conveniently been born even before the old town had drowned. In 1893 a community election transferred legal title to the new Amarillo which was already boasting a population of 482 hardy survivors.

Two more railroads promptly came to the booming little town and new highways soon reached it, paralleling the tracks of the railroads. By the early years of the twentieth century, Amarillo had become the transportation hub of the Panhandle. Cattle raising, farming, and petroleum production soon brought a respectable degree of wealth to what only a short time earlier had been nothing but barren prairies known mainly for the freakish and often extreme patterns of weather that prevailed there.

Aside from its weather, travelers to the Texas Panhandle have always been quick to observe that the distances to it and within it seem immense. Amarillo, for example, is closer to the capital cities of three other states than it is to its own capital in Austin.[4] Although railroads and highways had served to drastically reduce travel times in the Panhandle as compared to the earlier days of horseback, stagecoach, or buggy, a journey to or from Amarillo, located at the heart of the region, continued to seem no less interminable until aviation came of age in the early 1900s.

The first aircraft to reach Amarillo were two U.S. Army biplanes that arrived in the city on April 27, 1918. The excitement surrounding their arrival made it quite apparent to the city's leaders that aviation held great potential value for their remote community, and the chamber of commerce initiated an aggressive campaign to persuade commercial airlines to provide regular service to their city that was so painfully far from everywhere. Aviation fever gripped Amarillo even more profoundly following Charles Lindbergh's much publicized epic flight from Long Island to Paris in 1927. As a local newspaper saw it, if airplanes could safely fly across the Atlantic Ocean, they should be able to make it across the vast reaches of the Texas Panhandle to serve the region's principal city on a regular basis.[5] In farsighted anticipation of the day when aviation would indeed become a widely accepted mode of transportation, Amarillo resolved to be prepared. As a result, there were five airports serving the city by 1932 with English Field designated as the city's official municipal airport.

Five years later, English Field was being served by several major interstate airlines that connected the Texas Panhandle with several other out-of-state airports. With the advent of regularly scheduled air service, Amarillo expanded its importance as the transportation hub of the entire region, which it had been since 1893. The winds of war, however, would soon bring even greater aviation excitement, activity, and prosperity to the region.

A WAR COMES TO THE PANHANDLE

The United States Army Survey Party here last night brought to Amarillo the most thrilling news it has had in years.

Amarillo News-Globe
September 10, 1941

What a gathering it must have been at the venerable old Herring Hotel in downtown Amarillo that autumn night over a half-century ago! Army Col. W. T. Blackburn, chairman of the army's Air Base Site Surveying Team, had electrified Mayor Joe Jenkins and two dozen other civic leaders with the announcement that their city was being recommended by his team as the location of a $10 million airfield to be the home of a heavy bombardment group. With the imminent involvement of the United States in the war already raging in other parts of the world now a foregone conclusion, the army was going to need bases all across the country.

Acting upon a much earlier recommendation made by Gen. Billy Mitchell that Amarillo held great potential to become the center of a vast air combat region, the army had thoroughly surveyed the area and ultimately concluded that General Mitchell had indeed been right.

When asked by one local leader why other cities had already received the survey team's endorsement, Colonel Blackburn deftly brushed aside any suggestions that the Panhandle's reputation for having atrocious weather might have delayed a favorable decision to build an air base near Amarillo. With commendable candor, the colonel admitted that he did not know why it had taken so long to give the green light to the idea. "I knew there would be little trouble in locating a site out here," Blackburn claimed. "I have been lost several times in this country."[6] Just why its chairman's past history of being lost in the Panhandle skies should have prompted the survey committee to recommend Amarillo as the site for a bomber base was not publicly revealed at the 1941 meeting.

At any rate, the city rejoiced at the announcement. The prospect of the arrival of some 6,000 officers and men along with their families obviously elated local businessmen. The town's leaders rightly foresaw no difficulty in passing the $100,000 bond issue required to raise some of the funding necessary to satisfy the survey team's conditions for final governmental approval. The 3,200 acres of land that needed to be acquired and given to the army presented no foreseen barrier in an area noted for its inexpensive and wide-open spaces. The additional requirement that a three-lane highway be built to the proposed site could easily be met. According to Colonel Blackburn, all of these prerequisites were only "reasonable contributions by Amarillo to the cause of victory," albeit victory in a war that had not as yet actually commenced.[7]

Blackburn and his team revealed that sixty-nine B-17 bombers would be assigned to the base, practicing their bomb runs on a bombardment range of several thousand additional acres to be leased from area ranchers. To allay any apparently unexpressed fears on the part of his organization's members, the secretary of the Amarillo Chamber of Commerce assured the city that all bombs used "in such target practice would be duds—sacks of flour, sand, and sawdust."[8]

With his survey team's work completed and clearly a rousing

success, Colonel Blackburn and his staff departed for Washington to gain final official approval for his recommendation. Before leaving, he assured city leaders that the new installation, which was certain to be approved, would be a permanent one. He stated, "We do not believe the Air Force will recede after the emergency." As evidence of his confidence in the future of an enduring and amicable relationship between Amarillo and the army, Colonel Blackburn's parting words to his hosts were, "I know that we will enjoy living with you."⁹ Enthralled by visions of federal funds in great abundance and perhaps even more motivated by a patriotic fervor to help win the war whenever it came, Amarilloans also eagerly looked forward to living with the United States Army Air Force.

As usual, it took some time for the wheels of the federal bureaucracy to grind out its approval of the army site location team's recommendation of Amarillo. On November 29, 1941, only eight days before America's sudden entrance into the war, a local newspaper reported that "unimpeachable sources" had divulged that the final approval could be expected within another two weeks. However, the newspaper cautioned that, "If Moscow were to fall to the invading German Army and if Japan and America go to war," it would be highly likely that all tactical air bases then being planned for the continental United States "will have to wait development of bases which the Army will be compelled to establish quickly in the Philippines and the Aleutians."¹⁰

Dismissing the seemingly remote possibility that any worldwide military events could derail Amarillo's hopes for the promised big bomber base, the newspaper hastened to reassure its readers that the prospects for getting it were still bright. One "high-placed government official" was quoted as saying that the "Chief [Air Force Commanding General Henry H. Arnold] might almost immediately" demand that the issue of bomber base locations be resolved. "The chances are ten to one," said the unnamed official, "that Amarillo will be on that list."¹¹

Although General Arnold and his staff were taking their time in making their decision, the city of Amarillo had moved with great alacrity to live up to its end of the September 1941 agreement it had made with Colonel Blackburn. The $100,000 bond issue had passed by an overwhelming margin and an option had been placed on all of the required acreage at a reported $32.50 to $35 per acre. In addition, another 800 acres had been placed under option, making over 2.5 million square feet of Texas Panhandle wheat land now available for the Army Corps of Engineers to transform into a bustling air facility, as soon as the favorable word came from Washington. Amarillo was clearly ready and eager to go to war.

A WHEAT FIELD BECOMES AN AIRFIELD

When we get finished building this thing, it'll be bigger than Lubbock.

> Col. Edward C. "Red" Black
> First commanding officer
> Amarillo Army Airfield
> Quoted in *Amarillo News-Globe*
> April 2, 1942

The flamboyant Colonel "Red" Black and his small staff arrived in Amarillo from Sheppard Field, at Wichita Falls, Texas, on April 1, 1942, and immediately set up headquarters in the Amarillo Building downtown. Black had supervised the construction phase at Sheppard Field, and just prior to that accomplishment he had overseen the building of Chanute Field at Rantoul, Illinois, in record-breaking time.[12]

As it developed, however, the airfield that Colonel Black had come to construct in Amarillo was not going to be the huge bomber base that his fellow colonel, W. T. Blackburn, had announced in late 1941. The attack on Pearl Harbor only weeks after Blackburn's meeting with city officials had caused the War Department to create training bases in Texas instead of the tactical installations previously envisioned. Amarillo Field, General Arnold had finally decided, was now to become an Aircraft Technical School rather than the home base of B-17 bombers.

On April 20, just nineteen days after his arrival in town, Colonel Black ordered the Army Corps of Engineers to begin construction on what rapidly took shape as a major training facility.

Located just across the runway from English Field, the air base soon boasted nearly eight hundred buildings, including five huge hangars, seven training buildings, twenty warehouses, and a complete seven-hundred-bed hospital complex. Construction crews speedily completed work on twenty-seven miles of paved streets and twenty miles of water mains serving the over six hundred barracks that would soon house soldiers learning to maintain the nation's growing fleet of B-17s.[13]

Five chapels, three barber shops, eight post exchanges, and a motion picture theater, with tickets selling for just fourteen cents, soon stood where only months before had been fields of wheat. Sixty tennis courts, fifty-four softball diamonds, and a football field were built to provide recreation for the flight engineers and aviation mechanic-trainees who were scheduled to begin arriving in the Panhandle.[14]

On September 2, just five months after Colonel Black had himself arrived, the first training classes began at the airfield. The training went on around the clock, with four six-hour instructional sessions taking place seven days a week. Thousands of students were assigned to the airfield for the four-month-long course of instruction, with the first class graduating from the air mechanics school on December 23, 1942.

Apparently the relationship between the army's students and the citizens of Amarillo was a cordial one. Despite their rigorous training schedule, many soldiers found their way into the city, and cafes and motion picture theaters as well as churches welcomed the visitors warmly. The army seems to have shown a rare degree of forethought in the selection of the students to be sent to Amarillo Army Airfield. According to Colonel Black, most of the enlisted men assigned to the school would be from Texas, Oklahoma, and nearby New Mexico, with only a few from Arizona and California being picked. Black also assured the community that the students bound for Amarillo would not be "of the underprivileged and illiterate section of humanity."[15]

The people of Amarillo were fascinated by their gigantic new neighbor to the east and flocked onto the air base every time an invitation to do so was issued. The field's first open house was held on Armistice Day 1942, even before all of the construction work had been completed. On that occasion, nearly 40,000 people came from all across the region for a firsthand glimpse of the vast military city they previously could only view from afar.

Later in the war, the army air force staged an exhibit in Amarillo's United Service Organization (USO) auditorium to further acquaint local civilians with military life. On display were such diverse instruments of war as a captured German Messerschmitt fighter plane, an army howitzer, and a solitary carrier pigeon from Camp Claiborne, Louisiana. The bird was eventually released from the exhibit and was last seen flying eastward carrying a message back to its home base. No record remains to indicate if the pigeon made its way safely through a rather violent thunderstorm that occurred just minutes after its departure from the auditorium.[16]

In August 1945, just days before the end of the war with Japan, Amarillo Army Airfield staged its most memorable open house. It was an event that is still fondly recalled by many long-time Panhandle residents who went to the field to see the giant B-29s that were now the prime weapon of the army air force. Ramps were built so that the civilians could actually look into the cockpits of the massive and heretofore top secret aircraft. The bomb bay doors stood open to provide the visitors with a glimpse of where the deadly bombs were carried before being released on enemy targets.[17]

There were marching and close order drill exhibitions, athletic events, a formal parade by the students, and a fly-over by several B-29s in formation. The event concluded with a concert and dance featuring the nationally known big band of Tony Pastor. Newspaper accounts estimated that nearly 25,000 visitors crowded the field that day, nearly 5,000 more people than called Amarillo home at the time.

Just a week after the popular open house on the base, the bomb bay doors of another B-29 opened high over Hiroshima, Japan, and World War II came to a fiery conclusion almost at once. In Amarillo, civilians and soldiers alike shared in celebrating the nation's victory and the key role they felt they had played in attaining it.

Despite Colonel Blackburn's optimistic prophecy of 1940 that Amarillo Airfield would be a permanent installation, it was soon announced that with the coming of peace, the field was to be closed in the summer of 1946. Many of the buildings were sold and moved off the base, and some of the remaining hangars were leased as storage facilities for wheat, the very crop that had once flourished where until only recently B-29 engines had roared. The many thousands of military men and the 2,000 WACs assigned to the facility were transferred to other bases or discharged, and soon there was only one man left on the sprawling 4,000 acres that had once been Amarillo Army Airfield. As a city employee, the man's job was to patrol the grounds and watch for fires. Unfortunately, one of the deserted hangars did catch fire soon after the hapless patrolman had assumed his lonely duty. As the official watchman, he could only watch as the large building burned to the ground.[18]

A SECOND LIFE FOR AMARILLO AIRFIELD

I lived just down the road from the old air base from 1947 until late 1952. Some nights, when it was real late, I swear I could hear a B-29 engine sort of cough and then begin to roar. It was really kind of spooky.

> Lloyd P. Westermann
> Amarillo, Texas
> October 1998

Toward the end of his stint as a neighbor to the Amarillo Airfield, Mr. Westermann was no longer merely imagining that he heard the unmistakable sounds of aircraft engines. Late in 1951, the very real whine of jet engines filled the air east of Amarillo, replacing any imaginary rumblings from a ghostly B-29. With the coming of the Korean War in June 1950, the United States Air Force was suddenly and urgently once again in the market for aircraft engine mechanics. As a result, a jet fighter engine school was soon in operation on the old field which had been speedily refurbished and proudly renamed Amarillo Air Force Base. All of the stored wheat was hurriedly trucked out of the few surviving hangars, new barracks and elaborate recreational facilities were constructed, and by November 1951, the city of Amarillo was once again wholeheartedly in the military aviation business.

At the base's dedication ceremony marking the return of the air force to Amarillo, over 80,000 civilians poured through the front gate in less than three hours. The overwhelmingly successful open house was deemed by the Amarillo Chamber of Commerce as having been "The Outstanding Event of 1951."[19]

Not generally known for making conservative statements, the chamber in this instance may well have understated the true importance of the reopening of the air base. From its dedication in 1951 until it was again closed in January 1968, the base had an enormous economic and social impact on the city of Amarillo. Over the span of its second life, the base was at various times home to several mechanic training schools, assorted missile and radar units, and an operational squadron of the Strategic Air Command (SAC). Over 100,000 flight mechanics graduated from the base's technical schools and mighty B-47s, B-52s, and KC135s later roared from its new long runway into Panhandle skies.

Millions of federal dollars flowed into the regional economy from payrolls and from the ongoing massive construction projects that provided hundreds of well-paying jobs to area workers. At its peak nearly 17,000 individuals, both civilian and military, were employed on the base itself. Nearly $80 million had been invested in the facility over the years since the war, and its size had expanded to encompass nearly 5,000 acres. In recognition of the economic and military importance of the base, air force Gen. Nathan F. Twining announced in 1954 that Amarillo Air Force Base was to be a permanent installation. This was, of course, welcome news to the over 30,000 Amarilloans who held related support jobs off the base and to the thousands who were employed on it.[20]

Naturally enough, the entire region was stunned when the Defense Department announced in 1964 that the base was to be phased out despite all previous assurances to the contrary. As shocking as the news was, there was at least a hint of a silver lining in the further disclosure from Washington that all of the base's buildings and land would again become the property of the city when the facility was ultimately closed in 1968.

Amarillo moved swiftly to capitalize on the gift from the federal government. In 1971, a new municipal air terminal was opened taking advantage of the thick 13,500-foot-long, 300-foot-wide runway that had been built to accommodate SAC's heaviest bombers at a cost of $17 million. Deserted hangars were leased to general aviation companies and various technical educational enterprises moved into the training facilities left vacant by the departing air force.

Apart from the air terminal complex, however, most of the base's buildings that long ago survived the auctioneer's gavel and the bulldozer's blade now stand empty. The distinctive twin water towers still loom over the mostly deserted vastness, their once brilliant checkerboard paint design all but obliterated by the relentless sun and wind. Fifty-year-old buildings, windowless and decaying, are connected one to the other by crumbling sidewalks and weed-choked streets.

Across the still very busy runway that once launched the giant aircraft of war, Amarillo's modern air terminal hums with activity. Close to the terminal, however, buried beneath the airport's gleaming fire station, is an eerie vestige of the area's military aviation past. Behind a sturdy and heavily secured door, seldom used stairs lead down to the musty remains of a long abandoned SAC command post. Tables and chairs, thick with dust, still furnish quarters once occupied by flight crews on standby alert. Cockroaches and rats now scurry about where, long ago, crewmen under SAC's very strict orders to be airborne in a matter of mere minutes raced to their aircraft parked on hardstands located just outside.

Today, on those now empty hardstands there remain primitive cartoon-like figures of men, women, animals, and, of course, airplanes, each indelibly sketched onto the concrete years ago by bored air force security guards who used sticks as pens and sun-melted tar as ink. In some ways, the graffiti is no less poignant than the pictographs drawn long ago on the walls of cliffs by other bored sentinels from other civilizations. If nothing else, the sketches are among the very few unaltered tangible relics of a time when military aviation was an important and vital aspect of everyday life on the high plains of the Texas Panhandle.

A group of aviation cadets arrive at Pecos, Texas, by train, probably in 1944.
— Courtesy, West of the Pecos Museum, Pecos, Texas

Cadets pass in formal review at Pecos Army Airfield.
— Courtesy, West of the Pecos Museum, Pecos, Texas

A typical spring day at Pecos Army Airfield early in the war.
— Courtesy, Bill Davenport, Pecos, Texas

Another equally typical spring day in Pecos.
— Courtesy, Bill Davenport, Pecos, Texas

*This warehouse is one of the few original buildings left in place
at the site of Pecos Army Airfield.*
— Author's photograph

*Once the home of Billie Sol Estes, this house was built on what was the
swimming pool for black troops at Pecos Army Airfield.*
— Author's photograph

The Pecos city fire department facility as it appeared in 1998. The building was moved into town from the airfield in 1946 on B-29 tires.
— Author's photograph

Now the "El Suavecito" cantina in Pecos, this building was the NCO Club on the airfield during the war.
— Author's photograph

In 1942, work began on what would become Avenger Field near Sweetwater, Texas.
— Courtesy, Pioneer Museum, Sweetwater, Texas

The entrance to Aviation Enterprises at Avenger Field, the WASP flight training base.
— Courtesy, Texas Woman's University, Women's Collection, Denton, Texas. Used by permission.

The WASP on parade at Avenger Field.
— Courtesy, Pioneer Museum, Pecos, Texas

Three sisters in arms pose in front of the Walt Disney designed "Fifinella" WASP insignia.
— Courtesy, Pioneer Museum, Pecos, Texas

A WASP takes to the air in a PT-13 over West Texas.
— Courtesy, Pioneer Museum, Pecos, Texas

At completion of their ground school, WASP trainees rush to ring the old firebell in celebration at Avenger Field.
— Courtesy, Texas Woman's University, Women's Collection, Denton, Texas. Used by permission.

The WASP took survival training at the local Sweetwater town pool.
— Courtesy, Texas Woman's University, Women's Collection, Denton, Texas. Used by permission.

With no pool available on the base, the WASP created a beach environment out of Texas dirt and Army chairs.
— Courtesy, Pioneer Museum, Sweetwater, Texas

*Gen. Hap Arnold
contemplates the proper
way to present wings
to a WASP.*
— Courtesy, Pioneer Museum,
Sweetwater, Texas

*At the wishing well, WASP
candidates are shown clad
in their ill-fitting "zoot
suits."*
— Courtesy, Pioneer Museum,
Sweetwater, Texas

Women Air Force Service Pilots march in a Sweetwater town parade during the WASP reunion of 1972.
— Courtesy, Texas Woman's University, Women's Collection, Denton, Texas.
Used by permission.

Sleek B-29s crowd the ramps on Amarillo Field.
— Courtesy, English Field Air and Space Museum Archives, Amarillo, Texas

Military Police conduct a security check at the Amarillo Field open house, 1945.
— Courtesy, English Field Air and Space Museum Archives, Amarillo, Texas

Nearly 50,000 visitors attended the August 1945 open house at Amarillo Field.
— Courtesy, English Field Air and Space Museum Archives, Amarillo, Texas

Temperatures nearing the century mark did not discourage airfield visitors in August 1945.
— Courtesy, English Field Air and Space Museum Archives, Amarillo, Texas

A formal pass in review and an aerial formation are a highlight of the open house at Amarillo Field.
— Courtesy, English Field Air and Space Museum Archives, Amarillo, Texas

Young Texans pause to consider a machine of war at Amarillo Field's open house in August 1945.
— Courtesy, English Field Air and Space Museum Archives, Amarillo, Texas

The big band sound of the Tony Pastor Orchestra fills an Amarillo Airfield hangar late in the war.
— Courtesy, English Field Air and Space Museum Archives, Amarillo, Texas

The Strategic Air Command reactivated Amarillo Airfield as an Air Force Base in 1957.
— Courtesy, English Field Air and Space Museum Archives, Amarillo, Texas

B-52s line the ramp at Amarillo AFB, with the huge SAC-built runway at the left of the photo. The old Amarillo Airfield is shown in the background.
— Courtesy, English Field Air and Space Museum Archives, Amarillo, Texas

*Once the centers of activity, many now deserted hangars remain
standing at Amarillo AFB.*
— Author's photograph

A classroom at Amarillo AFB is now an empty shell.
— Author's photograph

By 1998, the twin water towers at Amarillo AFB had all but lost their traditional checkerboard paint jobs.

— Author's photograph

Across the runway, the catacomb of a long abandoned SAC Command Post lies deep beneath Amarillo Air Terminal's fire station.

— Author's photograph

Bored aircraft sentries drew cartoon figures on Amarillo AFB's hardstands using tar melted by the scorching sun.
— Author's photograph

A cartoon Tweety Bird character stares from an Amarillo AFB hardstand, drawn long ago by an air policeman with apparently little else to do.
— Author's photograph

A Texas cowboy was sketched in tar many years ago at Amarillo AFB.
— Author's photograph

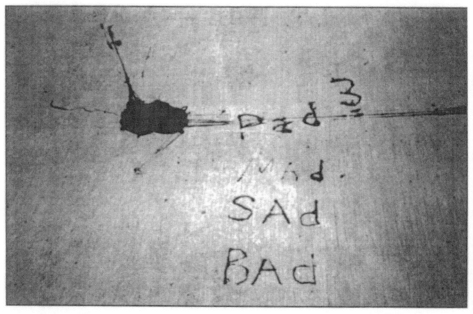

A disgruntled sentinel on Pad 3 summed up his attitude about guard duty in this tar drawing.
— Author's photograph

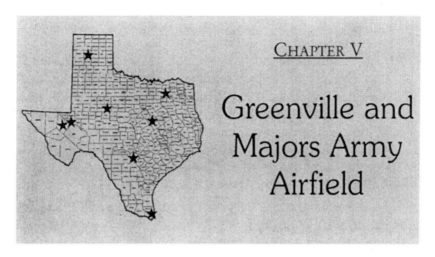

CHAPTER V

Greenville and Majors Army Airfield

Greenville is known nationally as the city of the blackest land and the whitest people.

Texas Almanac and State
Industrial Guide,
1939-1940

The nearly always reliable *Texas Almanac* apparently found nothing out of the ordinary in Greenville's national reputation as it existed in the year just before the outbreak of World War II.[1] After all, as the publication's editors most likely knew, a large sign reading "Welcome • Greenville • The Blackest Land • The Whitest People" had stretched over Lee Street in the city's downtown district since July 1921. People entering the East Texas town on U.S. Highway 67 were greeted by the sign as were other travelers who passed through on the trains of the Missouri, Kansas, and Texas Railroad.

The message that was so boldly printed on the sign had become something of an unofficial slogan for Greenville soon after it was unfurled. A local bank had imprinted it on the free checks provided to its customers, and one high school class had proudly engraved the slogan on their senior class rings. Travelers curious about the sign and its meaning could simply address their letters of inquiry to "The

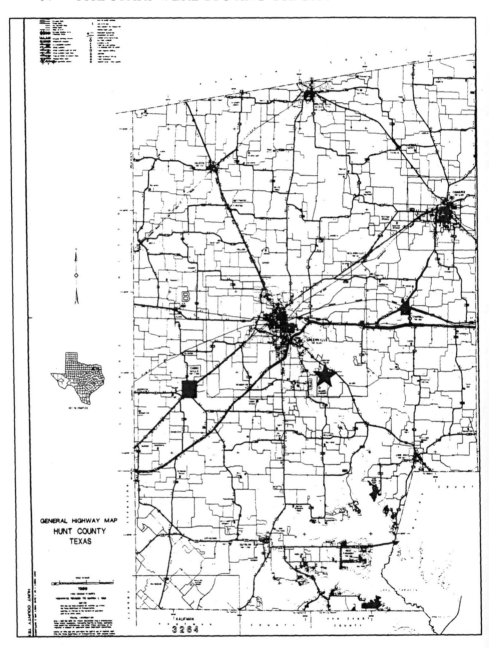

Hunt County Map
This map of central Hunt County shows the location of Majors Army Airfield during the war years. An inset map of Texas shows the location of the county within the state.

Blackest Land, The Whitest People, Texas," and the envelopes would be forwarded directly to the Greenville Post Office.[2]

Differing opinions about what the famous message truly implied triggered rancorous debates that continue to this day, even though the sign itself was taken down nearly thirty years ago largely at the insistence of Greenville's African-American leaders. Many longtime residents emphatically contend that there was absolutely no racial implication intended in the sign's message. It was, they argue, simply a proud testimony to the richness of the area's black and fertile soil, and the sterling and unbesmirched human qualities of the local inhabitants, be they black or white. Other townspeople, including many in the African-American community, have historically taken strong exception to this interpretation of the message.

Regardless of how the sign itself was being perceived in 1940, there can be little question that Greenville and all of East Texas were still racially segregated when World War II came to America the following year. Two distinct societies, one black and the other white, warily co-existed throughout the region, and the barriers separating the two were clearly defined and vigorously maintained. In many ways, the situation had been directly created by the Civil War. Hunt County, with its county seat at Greenville, had been almost exclusively an agricultural economy since its establishment in 1846. Although most of its many small farms raised cattle, corn, and other vegetable crops, a small but somewhat elitist group of slave-owning cotton planters wielded a disproportionate degree of political and social influence within the county.[3]

In 1861, likely to the delight of its cotton planter aristocracy, Texas voted to secede from the Union to become one of the eleven Confederate States of America. During the great Civil War that soon followed, many men from Greenville and Hunt County served in the Confederate armies.

When the tide of the war turned against the Confederacy in 1863, many cotton planters in other Southern states hurriedly began to move their slaves to East Texas, out of the path of the advancing Union forces. As a direct result, the slave population of Hunt County grew rapidly, nearly doubling by 1865. With the collapse of the Confederacy that same year, all slaves everywhere in the reunited nation were pronounced free and also given the right to vote.[4]

The stage was thus set for the racial unrest and strictly enforced policies of segregation that were to endure for decades in many parts of the South. The white majority in East Texas vainly sought to restore and maintain the traditional antebellum racial balance. Their efforts to do so often produced violent results and generated a climate of intolerance and mistrust that still prevailed when World War II started in late 1941.[5]

According to the *New Handbook of Texas*, lynchings were common occurrences throughout East Texas in the early years of the twentieth century.[6] Greenville itself experienced a violent racial incident in 1908 when an apparently falsely charged black man was taken from his jail cell by a white mob and burned to death on a city street. Although the murder was committed by a very small number of men, the nationwide publicity stemming from the event served to scar the city's reputation for years to come. The subsequent placing of the well-publicized "Welcome to Greenville" sign over Lee Street thirteen years later understandably did precious little to erase the scars. While troubled race relations were by no means unique to Greenville in particular, or East Texas in general, few if any other cities saw fit to publicly display such a controversial and easily misinterpreted sign that only tended to lend more fuel to the racial unrest.[7]

Following the Japanese attack on Pearl Harbor, the citizens of Greenville, both black and white, supported their nation and its war effort enthusiastically and with great patriotism despite their differences. World War II was to bring many hardships, of course, but in the final analysis, the conflict also proved to be an enduring social and economic blessing to Greenville, Texas.

MAJORS ARMY AIRFIELD

We was hungry!

W. A. (Cap) Caplinder
Greenville, Texas
October, 1998

Although there were serious social problems in Greenville when the war started, the condition of the economy was even more critical. As was true in nearly all sections of the United States in the late 1930s, East Texas was hard hit by the Great Depression. The demand for farm products had greatly diminished because of the nationwide economic downturn. With nearly 70 percent of the population living on its 5,891 farms in 1940, Hunt County's per capita income had dropped significantly and prospects for any immediate improvement were dim at best. At the depth of the depression, 2,259 people were on the county's relief rolls, and nearly 17 percent of the population was unemployed. Only 685 individuals in Greenville could be classified as wage earners with steady, non-agrarian jobs. Perhaps even more significantly, county records showed that the number of farms had dropped by 1,500 since 1930.[8]

Nearly desperate to find a way in which to bring much needed dollars to the area, the Greenville Rotary Club launched a campaign to obtain a municipal airport for the city. Reasoning that the construction of such an air facility would bring new money to the community, the organization petitioned the federal government in 1938 to consider Greenville as a site for a new airport. Preliminary studies were sufficient to stimulate initial federal interest in the project and in 1939, the Greenville Chamber of Commerce was encouraged to present its airport proposal to the CAA. The chamber's timing could not have been better. Greenville's airport petition happened to coincide with the massive federal effort to construct airfields all across the United States to create sites for the eventual training of flight crews. America's air forces had just been given a mandate to expand substantially and the army was clearly going to need many new training bases.

As it developed, Greenville's bid for a government-funded airport had an effective spokesman in Sam Rayburn, the district's powerful congressman. Rayburn used his influence to convince the CAA officials that six hundred acres of land then under option to the city of Greenville would be a prime location for a new airport.

In June 1941, the CAA inspectors visited the site, and in August, Rayburn notified an elated chamber of commerce that Greenville had indeed been chosen to receive federal funding for airport construction.

In order to get the $410,000 in funds that the federal government had promised, the city needed to exercise its options on the land, which had been expanded to 740 acres in size, and bring utilities to it. A bond issue was quickly passed and $60,000 was raised to put the project in motion. In January 1942, not thirty days after the attack on Pearl Harbor, construction began on the new base. At long last, the depression was receding from Hunt County. Its citizens were elated, and according to the *Greenville Evening Banner,* they "eagerly anticipated the wealth that comes from huge construction contracts."[9]

The coming of war had put airport matters into a different perspective. Although ostensibly funded by the federal government to be a municipal airport, America's entry into the conflict speedily transformed the Greenville project into a massive military undertaking. On April 1, 1942, the hardworking Sam Rayburn announced that the civilian air facility already under construction would instead become an army airfield. Over five million more federal dollars had been appropriated for the Greenville project.[10]

Workers flooded into the city and the construction activity proceeded at an almost frantic pace. Only ninety days after the work had begun, an army headquarters was opened on the base and in August 1942, cadets, support troops, and aircraft began to arrive.

One of the more annoying problems that faced both the army men and the construction crews that continued working almost around the clock was the shortage of drinking water. One soldier who was assigned to the base later recalled that he and his comrades-in-arms often drank water belonging to the construction workers. When the contractor complained, an army officer arranged for the servicemen to have a supply of beer on hand at all times. Recognizing a good deal when they saw it, the soldiers gladly left all available drinking water for the civilian workers in favor of the unlimited and free beer.[11]

Huge runways were soon stretching across the legendary black land of Hunt County. In less than a year, the construction crews had also built a military city that, according to one source, was about half the size of Greenville itself. In addition to the runways, two hundred buildings were finished, including a hospital, a gymnasium, a post office, a theater, maintenance shops, barracks, a commissary, and two churches.[12]

When the citizens of Greenville were given their first opportunity to see for themselves what had been so swiftly built just five miles south of their town, over ten thousand of them visited the base. The airfield's open house was held on January 5, 1943, the first anniversary of the death of Lt. Truett Majors for whom the base was named. He had been the first serviceman from Hunt County to die in the war. The crowds flocking to the base's open house were so great, the Reverend W. O. Majors, father of the dead pilot, had to get assistance from the military police so that he could get through the traffic jam in time to give the benediction at the opening ceremony.[13]

The primary mission of the huge new base was basic flight training for aviation cadets. The young trainees flew B-13A aircraft and at the peak of the airfield's operations, over 250 of the planes were assigned to the base. The training program lasted for nine weeks. According to an account in the *Greenville Evening Banner*, the cadets' day started at 0600 hours, with flight training in the morning followed by "drills, athletics, and ground schoolwork" in the afternoon. As at most training bases during the war years, accidents did occur at Majors Field, occasionally resulting in fatalities. In all, there were 128 accidents, resulting in 32 deaths. In total, 5,604 aviation cadets were assigned to Majors Field during the initial period of the basic flight training mission. Performance standards were high and the schedule called for a total of seventy hours of flying time, at the rate of one hour per day for five days.[14]

As was often the case, navigation on cross-country flights seemed to cause many of the fledgling pilots serious problems. To orient themselves on such flights, lost cadets would often fly very low over railroad depots in order to read the identifying sign on the station's exterior. Celeste, Texas, located north of Greenville, had its name painted in exceptionally large letters on its depot, making it a favorite of temporarily misplaced pilots.[15]

Not all cadets could measure up to the rigorous schedule and demanding routine of military life, and the army did not take pity on those who washed-out of the program. When dismissed, the ex-cadet was compelled to push a wheelbarrow laden with his personal belongings through the ranks of his former classmates who stood at rigid attention as their failed comrade left the field in disgrace. Fortunately, however, only 6 percent of all cadets washed-out of the Majors Field training program, a record that speaks well of the 180 flight instructors who trained the young cadet pilots.[16]

Some of the cadets seemed determined to test the strict disci-

plines set forth by their instructors. Although flying at a dangerously low altitude over Greenville was a dismissable offense, such
incidents apparently occurred with some frequency. Perhaps Cadet
Carl H. Abrahamson might have escaped dismissal after flying just
above Greenville's rooftops one day had he not pushed his luck too
far by executing a barrel roll completely around a commercial air-
liner bound for Dallas. Both escapades were reported to base
authorities and Abrahamson soon found himself pushing his exit-
wheelbarrow rather than the joy stick of a B-13.[17]

In addition to the army air force's cadets, Majors also had a
complement of the WACs and in 1944, some of the WASP arrived.
No one seemed to know exactly what the WASP were supposed to
do and as a consequence, they usually did what the male pilots simply did not want to do. Often, they were driven to some farmer's
distant field to retrieve a plane that had been landed there in error
by a nervous, inexperienced cadet. Although the WASP were usually qualified flight instructors, it was believed that male trainees
would rebel at the prospect of being taught to fly by a woman.
Although not permitted to serve as instructors, the WASP did manage to log an average of fifty-five flying hours per month, usually as
test pilots and retrievers of downed aircraft.[18]

The men and women on the base were provided with excellent
facilities for recreation. There were complete athletic programs,
movies, clubs, and touring USO shows to relieve the stress of flying,
teaching, or maintaining hundreds of airplanes. When leisure pur-
suits on the base lost their appeal, however, the military personnel
took the opportunity to go into Greenville. Contemporary accounts
relate that for the most part, the citizens of the city got on well with
their military guests. Churches welcomed the soldiers and church-
goers often took the servicemen and women into their homes.

Reports of civilian and military clashes in the town were few.
However, one longtime resident of Greenville believed that the
townspeople were so pleased with the sudden prosperity that the
base had generated they simply looked the other way when what
previously had been unacceptable incidents occurred.[19]

Before the army came, Greenville had been a legally dry community where even dancing was frowned upon, and where prostitution was something only whispered about. As longtime resident
W. A. Caplinder remembered it, things changed rapidly when the

base opened. Illegal liquor arrived daily on the Katy Railroad in large wooden cases usually labeled "Housewares." In addition, several enterprising bootleggers would take the early morning train to Dallas carrying empty suitcases, only to return a few hours later with their luggage laden with whiskey to be sold to thirsty soldiers. Near the base stood an illegal but nonetheless wide-open saloon commonly known as "Ug's" out of tribute to its proprietor's less than handsome countenance. According to Caplinder, the liquor flowed freely at Ug's tavern, particularly on payday, and ladies of dubious character would somehow materialize to relieve a soldier of what cash he might have left after paying Ug for an illegal drink or two. The county sheriff's deputies, remembered Caplinder, not only knew of these illicit activities but may have shared in the profits that were realized at Ug's and other such establishments located throughout the county. The proprietors of the saloons conveniently received warning well in advance of any official-appearing raids staged by the deputy sheriffs.[20]

There is some evidence that the citizens of Greenville were a bit wary of the thousands of young men who had suddenly descended upon their city. Although the townspeople patriotically supported the military effort and eagerly welcomed the new prosperity that Majors Field had brought to the area, the relationship between the longtime residents and the newcomers was usually formal and somewhat cautious. What the soldiers did at Ug's and other such remote dens of iniquity was one thing, but attempting such shenanigans within the city limits was something altogether different. To guard against any obvious in-town violations of its long established rules of decorum, the city formed a liquor and venereal disease control board that worked in tandem with the airfield's provost marshal. Military police mounted a highly visible patrol in town, particularly on Saturday nights to discourage any lapses in behavior.[21]

Civilian social pressure also guarded against overt fraternization between young soldiers and high school girls. Any Greenville high school girl seen with a soldier from the airfield often found herself blacklisted, shunned by boys in the school, and not asked out on dates.[22]

When black soldiers went into Greenville from Majors Field, they encountered no greater animosity or more restrictions than the local black citizens had been facing for years. The city was severely segregated and the line between the white and black races simply was not crossed. The black soldiers sat in the balcony of the only movie house in town that would admit them at all, and only ate in those restaurants located in the black section of town which was known as the Flats. Occasionally, a Saturday night brought intra-racial trouble to the Flats if a black soldier might in some way upset the civilian routine within the segregated community itself. In one such incident, a black military policeman on duty in the Flats shot and killed a local black man late one night, but no charges were brought against him, and the soldier was soon conveniently trans-ferred to another installation and the matter was eventually forgot-ten. There is no evidence that the black soldiers themselves made any serious effort to change the way their race had been treated for many long years in Greenville, much of the rest of Texas, and throughout the South.[23]

Though the lines of segregation were still well defined between the black and white societies in East Texas in the early 1940s, a new social challenge was to come to Greenville. On November 29, 1944, the *Aguilas Aztecas* arrived at Majors Field from Mexico.

THE FLIGHT OF EAGLES LANDS IN GREENVILLE

We really didn't see all that much of those boys who came up here from Mexico, but they always seemed to be well-behaved and very friendly.

Marian Harris Brownlee
Commerce, Texas
November 1998

Late in 1944, the primary mission of Majors Field was changed from basic flying training to fighter pilot training. The clumsy BT-13s were replaced by the powerful Republic P-47s, the famed "Thunderbolt" fighter plane. It had a 2,000 horsepower engine, compared to the BT-13's 450 horsepower motor, and it was at the time the fastest aircraft in use by the army air force.[24]

With the new mission and the newly arrived aircraft came pilots from several other nations who were sent to Majors Field to learn to fly the powerful planes in combat against the Axis. Most notable among the foreign pilot groups to arrive in Greenville was the *Aguilas Aztecas*, the Aztec Eagles of the 201st Fighter Squadron of the Republic of Mexico. The squadron was composed of some three hundred pilots and their ground crews. They had been chosen for this once-in-a-lifetime assignment only after stiff competition had weeded out those who failed to measure up to the high standards established for what would become the only Mexican military force to see combat action in World War II.[25]

The 201st was actually organized long after Mexico had declared war on Germany on May 24, 1942. A series of sinkings of Mexican ships by German U-boats had finally provoked the declaration of war, but for many months Mexico had served as a loyal but passive ally in the war against the Axis. Such vital raw materials as oil, leather, and food were made available to the United States and other allied nations, but no armed Mexican military force was sent into the war zones.[26]

After considerable internal wrangling and external negotiations with the United States, Mexican President Avila Camacho was finally able to announce that his nation would at last become a full partner in the conflict, with the 201st *Escuadron* of the Mexican Expeditionary Air Force, the *Aguilas Aztecas*, taking its place alongside fighter squadrons of the United States Army Air Force in a theater of war.

On July 21, 1944, the squadron left Mexico as the first Mexican troops ever sent to fight on foreign soil. However, before they could fight on any foreign soil, or for that matter even fly over it, the Mexican pilots would first need to undergo flight training in Texas just across the Rio Bravo. After a brief indoctrination period at Randolph Field in San Antonio, the squadron was assigned to Foster Field at Victoria, Texas, where they arrived on August 6, 1944.

Of the original thirty-six pilots in the squadron, two washed-out during the ten-week course at Foster Field. While at the base, the pilots received nearly one hundred hours of in-flight instruction in AT-6 and P-40 type aircraft. It soon became obvious that language was a significant problem in the successful integration of the

Mexican squadron into the American air force. Less than half of the enlisted men spoke English and even some of the pilots had a limited knowledge of the language of their host nation. As the weeks passed, however, the Mexican aviators grew more proficient in English, but language difficulties continued to be a problem until the end of the war.[27]

On October 17, 1944, the Mexican pilots left Texas for Pocatello, Idaho, for what was intended to be their final training assignment prior to embarkation to a theater of war. As severe winter came to Idaho early that year, it soon became obvious that another base in a more moderate climate would need to be found for the 201st to complete its training. The decision was then made to send the entire group back to Texas, this time to Majors Field at Greenville.

The unit, including officers and enlisted personnel, left Pocatello by train and arrived at Majors Field on November 29, 1944. Life on the base seems to have been amicable enough, at least for the Mexican officers. They participated in social events with their American counterparts when they were not flying their P-47s. On weekends, however, most officers preferred to go to Dallas for recreation rather than stay in Greenville. Some of the Mexican troops said they felt that the people of Greenville were more suspicious of them than the citizens of Pocatello had been.[28]

One historian believes that the residents of the East Texas city were more confused about how to treat the Mexican visitors than actually suspicious of them. Historically, there had never been any question about the division between the black and white societies in Greenville, but the insertion of a third and unknown racial element into the mix presented a whole new set of challenges.[29]

The English-speaking officers apparently encountered few if any signs of racial discrimination. One such officer in fact dated a local girl whose father operated a service station in town. When not on duty, the pilot charmed the station's patrons by washing their car windows and checking the air in their tires. He eventually married the girl and took her with him back to Mexico City after the war.

Some of the squadron's enlisted men found it difficult to integrate into Greenville's social structure. One man was denied service at a local restaurant, but after the base commander interceded on his behalf, no Mexican soldiers were turned away again.

On the base, the training of the 201st proceeded steadily, and on March 18, 1945, the squadron departed Majors Field, enroute to the Philippines and assignment to the 58th Fighter Group of the 5th Air Force. From their base on Luzon, the Mexicans flew fifty-nine combat missions from June 4, 1945, to the end of the war in August, and five of the pilots were killed during the course of their duties. The survivors returned to Mexico as heroes and the toast of their justly proud mother country.[30]

A KEY TO THE FUTURE

Majors [Field] was one of the most important things in Greenville's history. It provided the threshold from an agrarian economy to an industrial one.

> Vincent Leibowitz
> Greenville, Texas
> October 1998

The word "threshold" is often used to describe the lasting influence that Majors Field has had on Greenville. Unlike many air bases that existed in Texas during World War II, Majors has left an obvious legacy of social and economic reform. Though such legacies are clearly evident today, it is doubtful that in its final days as a military air facility there was any reason to expect that the field would have much if any impact on the city's future.

Despite the efforts of Sam Rayburn and the local chamber of commerce, Majors Field was deactivated on July 15, 1945, even before the war had ended. Faced with this setback, Rayburn at once began pressuring the government to give the field intact to the city and county, and by early 1946 he had accomplished his task. Several ventures then moved onto the old base to capitalize upon Rayburn's success. Included in these ultimately unprofitable endeavors were a chicken hatchery, a leather company, a grocery store, and even a beehive manufacturer.

In 1953, it appeared as though the air force itself might be returning to occupy its old wartime facility. In an election campaign speech that year, Speaker of the U.S. House of Representatives Sam Rayburn promised his Hunt County constituency that Majors Field was scheduled to be reactivated as a jet training base at a cost of $4.6 million. However, such high hopes were soon dashed by a massive federal budget reduction effort.

The defeat of the reactivation proposal for Majors Field eventually proved to be positive for Greenville. Rather than again becoming an active air base and a facility that might at any time fall victim to federal budgetary constraints and changing political fortunes, the remaining buildings on the old field were instead leased to the Texas Engineering and Manufacturing Company. Through a series of corporate permutations, that company eventually became The Raytheon Corporation, and in 1998, it was Raytheon that dominated the economy of Greenville, Texas, and its surrounding area.

The city today boasts a population of 23,305 while Raytheon, a leader in aircraft and electronic manufacturing, employs over 5,000 workers. Private sources estimate the actual number of Raytheon employees as being closer to 8,000, reflecting the highly classified nature of some of the corporation's activities.

Hunt County's official historian, W. Walworth Harrison, writing in 1976, was perhaps the first to recognize the tremendous advantage the huge military base had given the community. "The building of Majors Field airport," he wrote, "proved to be the threshold for Greenville's long dreamed of industrial growth and payroll."[31] As evidence of Mr. Harrison's observation, there are now thirteen large Fortune 500 companies in the county where, before the war and before Majors Field, there were fewer than seven hundred individual wage earners in total.

In many ways, the coming of the airfield brought about other changes to Greenville and Hunt County that are perhaps as significant as the economic revolution that occurred there. The hard and previously impenetrable lines of racial segregation have blurred and largely disappeared. The famous, or infamous, sign is nowhere to be seen and if its message was ever intended to be racially derogatory or not is now moot, since the sign has been down for nearly thirty years. The army brought soldiers from many lands and of all races to Greenville during the war as well as men and women from every corner of the United States. To be sure, there was nothing altruistic in the army's methods. It was itself nearly as segregated as

Greenville, but the fact remains that because of the war, all manner of Americans and soldiers from other nations were suddenly infused into what had essentially been a closed East Texas social structure. As a result of that forced infusion, the old and traditional social and racial barriers began to weaken and eventually dissolve.

To a large degree, the fortuitous building of Majors Field was only accidentally the key to Greenville's prosperous future. The city leaders of sixty years ago who were in fact desperately seeking some way, any way, to bring their economically distressed little community out of the depths of the Great Depression were fortunate enough to acquire one of the federal airport building projects. The army airfield that ultimately emerged from that initially modest project proved to be a critical turning point in the city's history, reshaping and improving it forever.

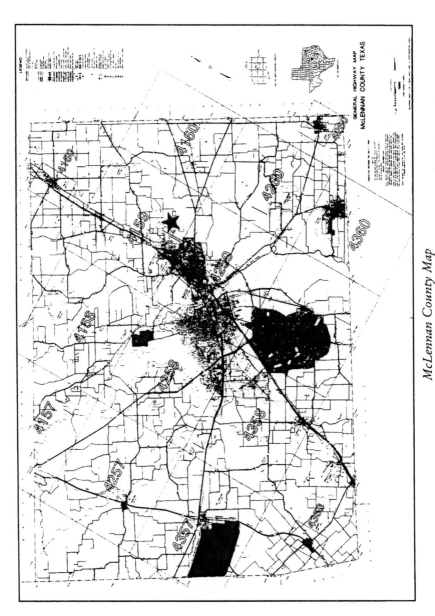

McLennan County Map

*This map of central McLennan County shows the location of Waco Army Airfield during the war years.
An inset map of Texas shows the location of the county within the state.*

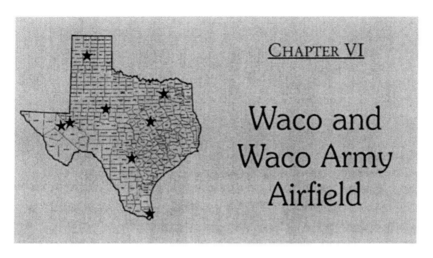

CHAPTER VI

Waco and Waco Army Airfield

Just as sure as I am sitting here, Waco will be bombed.

Col. William C. Torrence
City Manager, Waco, Texas
Quoted in the
Waco News Tribune
December 19, 1941

As it developed, of course, enemy bombers failed to appear over Waco, Texas, at any time during World War II. Although the city's fortuitous location not far from the heartland of America would seem to make it an unlikely bombing target, Colonel Torrence nevertheless took stern measures to ensure that the town he superintended was more than just adequately prepared for any wartime emergency that might possibly arise.

As a combat veteran of World War I, Torrence was all too well acquainted with the horrors of war. He could grimly envision what would happen to his historic city on the banks of the Brazos River should German, or Japanese, or maybe even Italian warplanes somehow manage to slip through the nation's air defense network to strike a deadly blow to Waco. Just a few days after Japanese planes had attacked the Hawaiian Islands, Colonel Torrence had completed meticulous civil defense plans that called for the entire

99

city to participate in a full-scale blackout test well-calculated to nullify the effectiveness of any such sneak air raid over Central Texas.

Torrence's test was by no means intended to be a surprise, as his office had made certain that all Wacoans clearly understood that on December 23, 1941, at 9:30 P.M. sharp, they were expected to extinguish any and all sources of illumination and remain in the dark, perhaps both literally and figuratively, until the all-clear whistles were sounded. Police and civil defense authorities would be on duty throughout the drill to ensure complete compliance and to sternly reprimand, and perhaps even arrest, anyone who failed to cooperate.

At the designated hour, Colonel Torrence picked up his telephone and dialed the secret encoded number that would set the entire operation into motion. Unfortunately, the colonel inadvertently entered an incorrect code and for several long and embarrassing minutes, all of Waco's bright city lights continued to burn in the late December darkness. When it became apparent to the citizens that the official whistle signaling the beginning of the blackout was not going to sound any time soon, they spasmodically commenced to turn their lights off anyway without the benefit of a city-provided signal. Soon, much of Waco was darkened.

One bright light from an office window, however, did serve to attract the attention of a police captain, and he hurriedly rushed through the otherwise dark building to locate and extinguish the offending lamp that possibly could, after all, serve as a guiding beacon for enemy bombers were they approaching the city. Much to everyone's chagrin, the violator of the stringent blackout regulations turned out to be none other than one Col. William C. Torrence, instigator and orchestrator of the late-starting exercise. Not only had he failed to launch the drill as scheduled, the colonel had also neglected to comply with his own guidelines.

Despite its shaky start, Waco's first and only blackout was deemed by some to be at least a modest success. Maj. John T. Sprague, the newly assigned commanding officer of the Waco Army Flying School facility that was still under construction north of town, watched from his circling airplane as the effect of the blackout slowly spread across the city. As military liaison officer for Colonel Torrence's otherwise strictly civilian undertaking, Major Sprague was not at all pleased by what he observed. Plainly visible from his vantage point in the air were the glowing tips of the multitudes of cigarettes being smoked in the darkness below by curious citizens standing outside their homes watching the spectacle of a city temporarily without illumination. Sprague realized that the tiny pinpoints of lights from thousands of burning cigarettes would provide clear evidence to even the most inexperienced of enemy bomber crews that a great many human beings were conveniently massed far below. Further, undimmed automobile headlights illuminated the roadways leading from all directions into what appeared from the air to be an almost totally black void highlighted only by glowing cigarettes and the briefly flaring matches being used to ignite them.[1]

Records show that Waco had no other blackout drills during the remaining years of the war, although a well-organized civil defense team remained intact until 1945. Major Sprague believed the first and only drill had been more or less a failure, while Colonel Torrence understandably rated it as a great success. Waco Mayor DeWitt T. Hicks took the political high road by simply observing that many problems had been uncovered in the course of the exercise.

All subjective assessments aside, the colonel's blackout, if nothing else, did effectively demonstrate to all Wacoans that they were indeed living in a country that was at war. Although Axis bombers fortunately never came anywhere near Waco during that war, the city did serve commendably as a vital air training center for thousands of army air force pilots who would eventually fly their bombers on deadly missions over Tokyo and Berlin.

WACO ARMY AIRFIELD

We grew a lot of cotton hereabouts, and when the Depression hit in the thirties, nobody nowhere had any money to buy cotton or anything else. Mostly, we planted vegetables where some of the cotton usually was, just so we could have something to eat.

Walter M. Granger
Waco, Texas
October 1998

As had frequently been the case in many other cities in Texas, leaders of the economically depressed city of Waco had urgently and routinely pressed federal officials to construct a major air facility near the city long before America entered World War II. On August 14, 1941, both city and McLennan County officials were elated to learn from the War Department that it would be willing to at least seriously consider Waco as the site for a large army airfield if the city would agree to acquire the required land for such a facility and then be willing to lease it to the federal government at the rate of one dollar per year.

Clearly aware of the highly beneficial impact that both the construction phase and an operational airfield would have on the region's all but dormant economy, the local officials sprang into action. A bond issue election to provide the necessary funds to buy the land was speedily organized. When the vote on issuing the bonds proved to be overwhelmingly in support, the city was in a position to secure title on a 1,162-acre parcel of suitable land situated some eight miles north of downtown Waco.[2]

Construction of the base soon began and millions of federally generated dollars flowed into the local economy. By early spring 1942, the rapidly built facility initially known as Waco Army Flying School was ready to welcome its first class of basic pilot trainees. Maj. John T. Sprague, the field's commander, had actually arrived in the Waco area in December 1941 just after America was thrust into the war. After personally observing the city's blackout episode with mild disgust, Sprague had supervised the construction phase of the airfield and had acted as an effective public relations representative for the army air force in Waco and throughout the surrounding area.

When he ceremoniously landed the first airplane on the field's just completed runway, John Sprague could not possibly have realized that he would make commanding the Waco Airfield his lifelong military career. A major when he arrived in Texas in late 1941, Sprague remained in command of what eventually became known as Waco Army Airfield until he presided, as a full colonel, at the facility's closing immediately after the war. Remarkably, Sprague again took command of the base when it reopened as a United States Air Force installation in 1948. He ultimately retired from the air force as a major general.[3]

On May 4, 1942, routine flight training operations began at the just opened airfield. At its peak in 1944, the base had a total of 5,000 officers, cadets, and enlisted personnel assigned to it. The city fathers who had so aggressively pursued the dream of a lucrative air base project for their community were undoubtedly highly pleased to receive the news that the facility's military payroll was exceeding $585,000 per month on average. Thus, the Great Depression began to fade in Waco and throughout McLennan County. In time, for most families it became only a very unpleasant memory.[4]

WACO AT WAR

I do remember that this town really got behind the army's airfields and everybody did all they possibly could for the boys out there and for the whole war effort in general. We all wanted to do something . . . anything . . . to help win that war.

Louise Marsh Timmons
Waco, Texas
October, 1998

Waco was one of the very few Texas cities to host two army flying schools during the war. Another instructional facility was opened later in May 1942 as a sub-base for Waco Army Flying School. Located some five miles northwest of downtown at Waco's Municipal Airport, the auxiliary installation eventually came to be known as Blackland Army Airfield. Townspeople extended a warm welcome to the personnel stationed at both bases and social events at the two fields were often the talk of the town.

The Girls Service Organization (GSO), a totally volunteer subsidiary of the national USO, spent many hours socializing with the soldiers at the airfields and at the USO club located in downtown Waco. On Sundays, members of the GSO were transported by army trucks to the airfields for an afternoon social hour. Each truckload of girls was supervised by a chaperone whose job it was to make certain that every one of her charges was safely back on board her assigned truck before it left the base on its return trip to town. Later in the war, the girls of the GSO were transported to the airfields for dances on Saturday nights. Even though travel was now by bus, the strict rules governing an orderly and well-chaperoned departure for the trip back to Waco continued to be enforced.

As was usually the case in all Texas cities that had military installations nearby, Waco's local churches extended a cordial welcome to the servicemen and provided them with much appreciated social contacts. As elsewhere, church-going families often invited the visiting soldiers into their homes for Sunday dinner following the services.

Waco's wholehearted support of the overall war effort was by no means limited only to Saturday night dances and Sunday suppers. Mrs. S. L. Elder, for example, found a particularly unique way to do her bit for victory. In order to raise money for Waco Army Airfield's athletic and recreation fund, she donated 450 pedigreed chicks from her Valley Mills hatchery. The young fowl were then sold for a nickel per head at Waco's Sears Roebuck store with all the proceeds flowing directly into the coffers of the base's recreation fund.[5]

Citizens without any chickens to donate bought war bonds instead. Early in the war, one special bond drive was organized for the express purpose of locally raising sufficient funds to make possible the outright purchase of a B-17 bomber. "In Waco, this is Bomber Week," proclaimed newspaper advertisements and hundreds of colorful posters that were displayed throughout the city.[6] Even though the announced sticker price of a B-17E in 1942 was a then astounding $278,000, patriotic Wacoans exceeded the goal by purchasing almost $380,000 worth of war bonds during the week of April 24th. Five months later, as a result of the successful bond drive, a brand new Flying Fortress rolled off the production line at Boeing's assembly plant in Seattle bearing the proud title of "The City Of Waco, Texas," in honor of the town that had paid for it. Other war bond drives conducted in the community during the war raised enough money to completely fund the building of five more airplanes, a torpedo boat, and two giant transport ships.

The city's younger citizens enthusiastically did their part in helping win the war. Four hundred and thirty-five east Waco school children mounted a massive scrap metal collection drive that by the end of only one week had yielded well over 12,000 pounds of discarded metal items. Melvin A. Lipshitz, a local junkman with both an obvious flair for statistics and an apparent access to classified army specification data, estimated that the collected metal could be recycled and transformed into "240 fifty-caliber machine guns, 24 one-ton bombs, 12 seventy-five millimeter field guns, or 2 three-inch antiaircraft weapons."[7] Joe Chapin, a prominent area farmer, found nearly as much scrap metal in his barn in one day as the schoolchildren had been able to collect in a week. He was understandably more than pleased to donate it all to the war effort while tidying up his barn a bit at the same time.

Waco's Baylor University also played a significant role in winning the war. Many of its male students enlisted in reserve officer training courses on the campus and coeds received full college credit for attending war-related technical classes. University president and former Texas governor, Pat Neff, fully endorsed the military activities at Baylor even though some alumni were less supportive. "At times," said Mr. Neff, "we need to fight as well as pray."[8] In an apparent effort to give his students more time for both fighting and praying, in 1942, Neff ordered the school's athletic department to suspend Baylor's football program for the duration of the war. It was the only school in the Southwest Conference to take such action. On March 6, 1945, in recognition of all of the university's wartime efforts, a newly built transport ship was christened the "S.S. *Baylor Victory*" in ceremonies at a shipyard in Wilmington, California.

Five months after the big ship went to sea, World War II came to its victorious conclusion. Wacoans and servicemen alike joined the rest of the nation in a jubilant celebration of the end of the war. Although the long and costly conflict had too often brought grievous personal loss to many Waco homes, it had also proved to be a powerful stimulant to the community in general. McLennan County, for example, had recorded a 365 percent increase in industrialization from 1942 through 1945 with a commensurate increase in per capita income. The population of Waco proper had increased by over 50 percent, growing to nearly 85,000 by the time the war ended.[9]

Waco Army Airfield had compiled commendable statistics as well. Twenty-nine classes of basic pilot cadets had graduated from its training program and over 750,000 hours of flying time were logged during the thirty-nine months the field was operational. In addition, 236 pilots from South and Central America had acquired their basic flying skills in Waco.[10]

Early in September 1945 with the war just over, Waco Army Airfield was placed on standby status. Shortly thereafter, the facility was fully closed, apparently forever. Waco's days as an important air training center seemed to be a thing of the past, but a military rarity was soon to occur.

THE SECOND TIME AROUND

When we heard that the airfield was comin' back, it was like a kid hearin' that Santa Claus would be comin' twice in one year. It was just too good to be true.

Martin Overman
McGregor, Texas
November 1998

Just three years after it had been placed on standby status and without any shooting war to prompt such an action, the old airfield was returned to full operation, first as Waco Air Force Base and then as Connally Air Force Base. Finally, in 1950, the name of the facility was changed for the last time to James Connally Air Force Base (JCAFB), with the ubiquitous John T. Sprague again in command. The initial mission of JCAFB was to train pilots, but by June 1951, the mission was changed to the training of navigators, radar observers, and bombardiers. Over the next decade, the base continued to instruct flying personnel, including many from foreign nations.

At its operational peak in 1963, JCAFB had a population of 3,523 military personnel and 826 civilian employees. In 1965, its combined payroll was nearly $31 million per year, representing over 10 percent of the total income of all McLennan County. Since World War II, the base's area had nearly doubled and now contained 2,228 acres with 114 permanent buildings and over 1,000 housing units. Its two main runways were nearly 10,000 feet in length. Clearly, JCAFB was a formidable installation, in size as well as in federal dollar investment and economic importance. It was, according to one scholar's thesis, the largest industry in the entire area at the end of June 1965.[11]

Despite the base's obvious value, it was nevertheless targeted for closure by the Defense Department in 1965. Rumors of the intent to deactivate the base filtered out of the nation's capital long before the official announcement was made. In Waco, base officials dismissed all such rumors and indeed announced over $5 million of new construction projects for the facility, including $1.5 million in runway extensions and another $1.5 million to rehabilitate military housing units located near the base.[12]

Local investors, reassured by the federal spending programs and once again confident of the future of the huge base, invested heavily in land and construction projects nearby. In late 1966, however, the earlier rumors became shocking reality and JCAFB was ordered closed, this time permanently. Property values in the vicinity of the base plummeted and the recent private investors in JCAFB-fueled speculation reportedly lost great sums of money.[13]

Curiously, it appears that once the base closure was announced, many of the city leaders of Waco seemed to be unperturbed. Air force base officials were apparently far more concerned about the economic impact the closure would surely have on the community than the civilians seemed to be. Although they appeared to genuinely deplore the impending closing, the air force leaders had no ready answer as to how Waco might cope with the loss of the multimillion-dollar payroll that JCAFB was generating, nor how the city could possibly replace the estimated $3.2 million being spent annually in area stores by personnel assigned to the base. As usual, there were no easy solutions.

Fittingly, the principal speaker at the graduation ceremonies of the last cadet navigator class to leave JCAFB was retired Maj. Gen. Benjamin D. Foulois, the very man who had first brought military aviation to Texas nearly fifty-five years before. The twenty-one cadets of Class 65-15 listened attentively as the eighty-five-year-old aviation icon related tales of his long career as an aviator. Then, with their own newly won silver wings proudly displayed, the young officers left James Connally Air Force Base and Waco for their new assignments. The city's long enduring relationship with the military thus came quietly to a close.[14]

The deactivated base, estimated to be worth as much as $200 million, became the property of Texas A&M University. In time, the facility became the Waco campus of the TSTC, the teaching institution that still occupies the old base and seemingly thrives there. New classrooms have replaced military barracks, and the fifty-year-old hangars now house technical training facilities.[15]

There is nothing of consequence to indicate that Waco Army Air Field or its successor, James Connally Air Force Base, ever existed on the sprawling site, and there are no historical signs or markers of any kind.

To more than just a few Wacoans, the news that a large air force facility once flourished just north of their city seems to come as a complete surprise. One otherwise well-informed librarian, locally born and probably in her late forties, listened politely for a request for information about the airfield before she asked just where such a base might have been located. She was clearly taken aback to learn that she was in fact standing squarely on it. "Well," she declared, rising swiftly to her own defense, "I was born here and I think somebody once told me that the air force had been around here somewhere a long time ago, but I didn't believe it until now." Indeed, the most noticeable remnant of Waco's military aviation past is the air force's traditional trademark red-and-white checkerboard painted water tower. It stands as a fading and obviously inadequate monument to the memory of those who lived and flew there so many years ago.

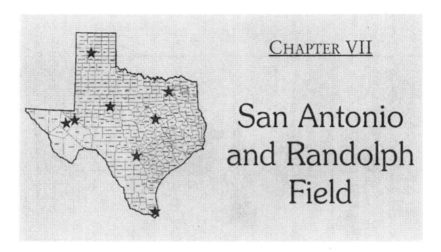

CHAPTER VII

San Antonio and Randolph Field

I had always heard that San Antonio was a great military town, but I didn't know just how true that was until I came down here from Chicago in 1942. There were guys in uniform everywhere in this city in those days, and somehow the folks hereabouts made each of us feel right at home.

Anthony Marschack
San Antonio, Texas
July 1998

Of all the cities in Texas, San Antonio was most likely the best suited to accept with warmth and enthusiasm the unprecedented increase in military activity brought about by World War II. As the capital of Spanish Texas and the historical setting for countless presidios, forts, and airfields since its founding in 1718, the city had long been witness to the comings and goings of throngs of soldiers wearing many different uniforms. Having often experienced actual combat within its municipal boundaries, San Antonio was truly a military town in every sense of the word.

The Spanish army had been the first to arrive, its exploration parties first reaching the area as early as 1691. A small village sprang up on the banks of the San Antonio River soon thereafter, and by

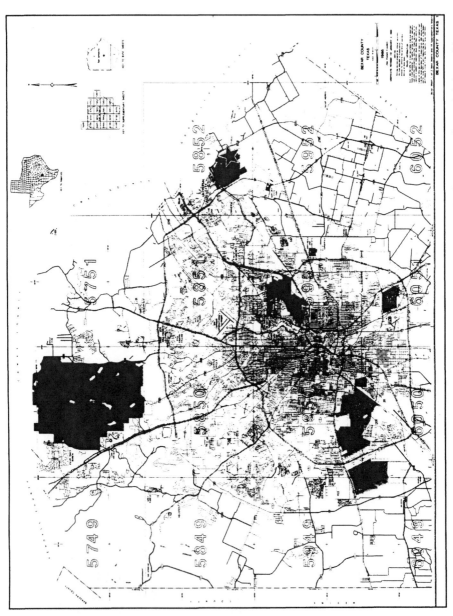

Bexar County Map. This map of northeastern Bexar County shows the location of Randolph Field. An inset map of Texas shows the location of the county within the state.

1778 the town was inhabited by over two thousand people. The early rapid growth of the *villita* reflected its importance as the first capital city of the Mexican state of Coahuila y Tejas.

During Mexico's struggle for independence from Spain in 1813, San Antonio declared itself free of Spanish rule, but Royalist forces held on to their northernmost state capital with a ruthlessness that all but decimated the population. Some twenty years later, the war for Texas independence from Mexico again saw violent military action in San Antonio, beginning with the Siege of Bexar in December 1835, and climaxing with the fabled Battle of the Alamo in March 1836. With the establishment of the Republic of Texas later that same year, the city retained much of its political prominence when it was named the seat of the newly created Texas county of Bexar.

As hordes of adventurers flowed into the new republic from the East in the late 1830s and early 1840s, San Antonio became the center for both the settling of South and Central Texas, and for the rapid expansion farther westward. A surprisingly vigorous military effort by Mexico to recapture the city saw two invasions by the Mexican army in 1842 and 1846 bring great destruction to the booming community. According to *The New Handbook of Texas*, the fear of future Mexican military action caused the permanent population of the town to plummet to just over eight hundred hardy souls shortly after the United States annexed Texas in 1845.[1]

When most apprehensions concerning any further significant Mexican military incursions were removed by its admission to the Union, Texas once again began to expand rapidly with San Antonio leading the way in the southern part of the state. By 1850 the population had grown to nearly 3,500, and by 1860, with a population of over 8,000, San Antonio was the largest city in the state. It was destined to claim this distinction for over sixty years.[2]

Although it was well on its way to becoming a major commercial and transportation center, in the early nineteenth century the city was still very much a military town. Several Indian skirmishes took place within the community's limits, and a large army presence was always garrisoned at various camps and forts throughout the immediate area.

In late 1860 and early 1861, as the probability of an American

civil war increased, Texas became aligned with other Southern
states. In February 1861, even before the Lone Star State had
seceded from the Union, local San Antonio militiamen forced
the surrender of the federal arsenal located in their city. Shortly
thereafter, U.S. Army Brig. Gen. David E. Twiggs somewhat in-
gloriously surrendered all Union forces and property within the
state of Texas to Southern forces, promptly earning him an angry
dismissal from the Northern army and a brand new commission as
a Confederate general officer.

During the four-year life of the Confederate States of
America, San Antonio continued to play an ongoing and important
military role, even though at least 40 percent of its citizens had
initially opposed secession from the Union. Many of its young
men were among the 90,000 Texans who saw service in the Civil
War, and the city itself was a major supply depot for Confederate
forces.

With the end of the war in April 1865, the victorious Union
Army returned to Texas, and San Antonio once again became its
headquarters. Although relations between the army and the community were often strained during the immediate postwar period of
Reconstruction, civic leaders were soon endeavoring to gain an even
greater degree of federal military activity for their city. These dili-
gent, vigorous, and for the most part successful civic efforts were
the beginning of a pattern that would in time make San Antonio
one of America's premier military centers.

It was an ex-Confederate colonel, one Thomas Williams, who
first put things into motion in an 1870 request to President Ulysses
S. Grant for $100,000 in appropriations to build a major army sup-
ply depot in the city. After much delay, the funds were approved
and, in further keeping with the civic-military pattern that was destined to continue, San Antonio generously deeded ninety-three
prime hilltop acres to the United States government in early 1875
for use as the site of the newly funded supply depot. In time, this
would become Fort Sam Houston and eventually the location of
the army's first significant aviation activities in Texas.

Upon completion of the fort, San Antonio was poised to maintain its military significance, although some of the names inscribed
on the new fort's commemorative plaque must have given many
die-hard former Confederates at least a momentary chill. First on

the list was the name of President Ulysses S. Grant, closely followed by that of General in Chief William T. Sherman and "Lt. Gen'l. Commanding, Division—Phillip [sic] H. Sheridan."³

Memories of former foes aside, the mere presence of the fort and its status as headquarters for the Department of Texas maintained and even amplified the strong military climate within the city. Some twenty years following the dedication of Fort Sam Houston, a war with Spain broke out. Over ten thousand Texans hastened to serve in that Spanish American War, with many of them eager to serve in Lt. Col. Theodore Roosevelt's colorful Rough Rider cavalry unit. Legend has it that some of the Rough Riders were boisterously recruited in the bar of San Antonio's Menger Hotel in May 1898.

With the Spanish-American War promptly and easily won, army life in San Antonio settled into the routinely drab day-to-day existence of peacetime. Fort Sam Houston continued to expand, however, with new and experimental missions being added to its operational programs.

On February 5, 1910, a diminutive former plumber and demonstrably fearless young army officer arrived at Fort Sam to inaugurate what arguably was one of the most significant experiments in modern military history. Little Benjamin "Benny" Foulois brought military aviation to San Antonio that day, albeit in a crate on a railroad flat car.

Foulois had served in the Spanish-American War and had distinguished himself during the 1899 Philippine insurrection by personally killing six Filipinos in hand-to-hand combat. Though small in stature, Foulois was clearly large in fortitude. Apparently tiring of close quarter fighting on the ground, he befriended aviation pioneers Orville and Wilbur Wright in order to learn more about their new flying machines. Following a ground school of less than one hour's duration, Foulois then taught himself to fly. As few other army officers had yet acquired this ability, the lieutenant soon saw to it that he was assigned to the Signal Corps in charge of the army's only existing aeroplane, a severely damaged Wright Model 1909-A.

When weather conditions in the East proved to be too unreliable for consistent air operations, limited though they were in those early years, Foulois was ordered to Texas and Fort Sam Houston.

As a result, San Antonio's bright and enduring future as a military air center was set in motion.

There were to be many mishaps between the arrival of Foulois and his train-borne aircraft and the eventual emergence of San Antonio as a major army aviation complex. Some of the more embarrassing early misadventures involved Foulois himself, piloting the grandly named but mechanically primitive Army Aeroplane Number One. On his first demonstration flight before hundreds of fascinated San Antonioans, Foulois, lying prone in the fuselage, nearly collided with a slow-moving automobile before finally crash-landing the flimsy craft. What one observer described as being a routine pattern had begun, one destined to be repeated for many months. Foulois and his Aeroplane Number One would be launched by catapult, fly for a few moments, only to crash-land once again. The pilot would then help carry the craft into a nearby garage for repairs. As his aeroplane had skids rather than wheels for landing purposes, such crash-landings were all but inevitable. Between flights, he would correspond with the Wright brothers seeking words of technical advice and then take to the air only to crash again on Fort Sam's broad parade ground. Included in the guidance given him by the famous flying brothers was to always stay with the aeroplane if trouble occurred in flight. Inasmuch as the parachute had not yet been perfected, this appears to have been sound advice.[4]

Lieutenant Foulois gamely persisted in his pattern of primitive flight attempts, and as a result of his diligence, the army eventually came to grudgingly accept the fact that airplanes might indeed be useful in military operations. By 1912, the War Department had accordingly approved the then huge sum of $125,000 for what was simply termed "Aeronautics."[5] America's military air force was thus formally created, thanks largely to the indefatigable Lt. Benjamin Foulois and his battered Wright Model 1909-A.[6]

The first aircraft procured with the newly appropriated funds was a Curtiss Type IV, fittingly dubbed Aeroplane Number Two by the army. Unfortunately, the service's second aircraft was even more unreliable than its predecessor. It was, in fact, to prove fatally dangerous.

On May 10, 1911, Lt. George E. M. Kelly, one of Foulois's students, attempting to land the new plane at Fort Sam Houston, brought the craft in at an unfortunately steep angle. The aircraft touched down but bounced sharply and took to the air again. Once airborne, it veered toward a long line of tents housing soldiers of the Eleventh Infantry. Somehow, Kelly was able to control his plane just long enough to avoid hitting the tents, but it suddenly nosed over and crashed, fatally injuring its pilot.

As a consequence of the crash and the near miss that had imperiled troops on the ground, Fort Sam's commanding officer banned all further flying activity at the fort. Having no other suitable place in Texas to train its fledgling aviators, the Signal Corps reluctantly transferred its one remaining airworthy plane back to College Park, Maryland.[7]

By early 1916, however, the indomitable Benny Foulois had returned, bringing more aeroplanes back to San Antonio. He was now a captain and commander of the newly formed First Aero Squadron. Stationed on the very parade ground at Fort Sam Houston from which he had been exiled five years earlier, Captain Foulois directed the activities of his fifteen pilot air force which shared the squadron's nine Curtiss Jennys and Burgesses. Disturbances along the Mexican border had brought about an increased military presence in San Antonio, with the First Aero Squadron being but a small part. In March 1916, the squadron was ordered into action with Brig. Gen. John J. Pershing's ill-fated Punitive Expedition along the Rio Grande.

Although Foulois and his pilots served willingly and bravely, their efforts to assist Pershing's ground forces were for the most part futile. The expedition's most significant contribution to the future of American airpower was the realization that based on the First Aero Squadron's ineffective performance, better aircraft and better flight training were sorely needed. Mute testimony to the validity of this conclusion was the undeniable fact that although not one of Foulois's planes had been even slightly damaged by hostile rifle or machine gun fire in Mexico, only three of his original nine aircraft armada had returned to San Antonio intact when the abortive Punitive Expedition was withdrawn.[8]

In August 1916, with the debacle of the First Aero Squadron still unfolding along the Mexican border, and the Great War in Europe intensifying, Congress recognized the need to enhance the army's aviation effectiveness and provided an astounding $13 million to the War Department to expand and improve its flight training, equipment, and facilities. By virtue of its existing prominence in military aviation, San Antonio was poised to benefit immensely from the government's sudden largesse.

Shortly after America's entry into World War I in April 1917, it was determined that a new and consolidated training facility would be established in San Antonio. Fittingly named Kelly Field in honor of the city's first military aviation hero, the field was completed and in full operation in just eight months' time. By December 1917, over 1,100 officers were undergoing flight training at Kelly Field.

When World War I ended, Kelly Field was one of the few flying schools kept open by the army, although at a greatly reduced level of activity. By 1922, however, the field was once again fully operational, having been designated the army's Consolidated Advanced Flight Training Center. Meanwhile, nearby Brooks Field had become the site for primary pilot instruction.

As the host city of the majority of the army's flying training programs, San Antonio had emerged as one of America's preeminent military cities by the late 1920s. Ironically, it was to be the city's expansion, fueled in part by its military importance, that would eventually lead to the establishment of yet another gigantic training base, the legendary Randolph Field, perhaps better known for decades as "The West Point of the Air." The story behind the birth of Randolph Field and San Antonio's bold bid to retain and even embellish its claim as one of America's principal military aviation centers is a tribute to both governmental heavy handedness and the power of dedicated civic endeavor.

A HIGH STAKES BLUFF AND THE BIRTH OF AN AIRFIELD

There can be no doubt about it whatsoever. San Antonio is now the crowning glory of the Army Air Corps, and Randolph Field is the brightest star in that crown.

The San Antonio Light
April 9, 1938

Due in part to its permanent military establishments that had survived the wholesale deactivations following World War I, San Antonio grew rapidly in both area and population from the end of the war through 1930. According to the U.S. Census taken that year, Bexar County's population had reached almost 300,000, nearly three times what it had been only twenty years before. San Antonio itself boasted a population of over 230,000, and the city was expanding in all directions into heretofore vacant county land. Located just five miles from downtown San Antonio, Kelly Field was directly in the path of urban expansion and soon found itself well within the city limits.[9]

Air Corps officials recognized that the flight training operations at Kelly and nearby Brooks Field did not mix at all well with everyday civilian activities. Rooftops, telephone poles, and water towers were clearly not compatible with low flying aircraft. Consequently, the army began a nationwide search for a new flight training facility site safely removed from urban growth and large enough to accommodate a consolidated training agenda. As might be expected, news of the government's desire to build a new base spread rapidly. Cities in Florida, California, and Louisiana made bids to the site selection committee. In Texas, Houston, Dallas, Fort Worth, and New Braunfels all touted their many attractions to army officials. Although the airfield site committee apparently listened attentively to the many presentations made by the rival cities, there is much evidence that the Air Corps wanted very much to stay in the San Antonio area, but at some new and less congested location.[10]

There were two reasons why the Army Air Corps wanted to stay close to the Alamo City, where it had been happily ensconced, at least off and on, since 1911. For one thing, San Antonio had historically nurtured its military population with great care, graciously accepting the soldiers as neighbors, and generously providing for them with a consistently warm exhibition of genuine Texas hospitality. Perhaps even as important, the flying weather in the skies above San Antonio was all but perfect. In fact, a later study of flying conditions would show that in a six-year period representing over two thousand days, only ninety-four of them were deemed unsuitable for flight training operations.[11]

Apparently overconfident about its proven qualifications as America's air training capital and therefore rather smugly little con-

cerned about the generous and enticing offers being made to the
army by other cities, San Antonio's civic leaders launched what
seemed to be only a half-hearted campaign to persuade the government to build another airfield nearby. As the city's expansion continued to encroach on Brooks and Kelly Fields at an ever accelerating pace, however, the army's patience with its present host city
began to grow thin. Brig. Gen. Frank P. Lahm, commander of all
Air Corps training operations, soon found it necessary to vigorously stimulate San Antonio's curiously sluggish efforts to formal-
ly propose a suggested site for the new base.

The general easily got the attention of the city's leaders when
he announced that they should be aware that if a suitable new site
was not soon forthcoming, the army would forthwith close both
Brooks and Kelly and leave San Antonio, probably forever. If this
news were not sobering enough, General Lahm also stressed that by
"suitable" he meant a site at least 2,000 acres in size, and by
"offered" he meant a tract of that magnitude being given free and
clear to the United States Army Air Corps. This dramatic demonstration of governmental heavy handedness took place in early
March 1927. Shortly thereafter, General Lahm added even more
fuel to inflame the agitation of the civic leaders when he further
announced that options on the amassed property had to be in his
hands before New Year's Day, 1928, a scant eight months in the
future.[12]

While the thought of not getting the highly desirable new base
was upsetting enough to San Antonio's leaders, the suddenly very
real possibility of losing the two extremely economically important
bases that already existed was more than the city's fathers could
even bear to imagine. Consequently, an almost desperate crash program was hurriedly put into motion under the auspices of the
Military Affairs Committee of the San Antonio Chamber of Commerce to immediately acquire a suitable airfield site.[13]

The army had made the finding of such a site even more chal-
lenging by stipulating that in addition to its enormous size, the plat
acreage had to be within five to ten miles of the city's existing limits, be served by a railroad and at least one good highway, and have
all utilities in place. Despite the seemingly impossible guidelines
and time constraints, the chamber's executives set to work careful-
ly and systematically, but understandably in great haste.

Within seven short months, the committee had put together a site near Calf Hill located just east of San Antonio that satisfied all governmental requirements. Options had been acquired on over 3,483 acres of land that belonged to several individual German farm families. Through the services of Ernest J. Altgelt, a chamber representative who spoke fluent German, the farmers had been persuaded to sell their property at market value and vacate what had been their traditional family homesteads. Unfortunately, one of the farmers, William Rittiman, decided at the last minute not to sell his tract of land, and as General Lahm felt that this particular piece of property was essential to the overall project, the entire Calf Hill site offer was rejected by the government. Undoubtedly disappointed but apparently undaunted, the chamber of commerce executives started their search anew, with General Lahm's New Year's Eve deadline drawing ever nearer.[14]

After considering nineteen other sites in Bexar County, options on a second viable parcel of 2,300 acres were finally secured. Again, the German-speaking Mr. Altgelt had been successful in convincing twenty-four other farm families to part with their land. This time, all of the owners were unanimous in their decision to sell. Located some sixteen miles east of San Antonio near the small town of Schertz, the property was situated on State Highway Number Three, was served by the Southern Pacific Railway, and all necessary utilities were readily available nearby and could soon be in place.

On New Year's Eve, 1927, San Antonio's relieved but elated civic leaders announced to the army that the site was officially being offered to the government, all guidelines concerning size, conditions, and time requirements having been faithfully met. The government accepted the offer at once, and plans for what eventually became Randolph Field began to take shape. If the federal government had been bluffing with its threat to close Kelly and Brooks in the event a suitable site for the new field could not be found, San Antonio had successfully called the bluff in this high stakes game. As history would show, both the city and the nation were the winners.

The only obstacle still to be overcome by San Antonio, however, was a formidable one. Somehow, within the strict legal guidelines concerning such matters, the city had to find the money to pay the farmers who had agreed to sell their land. The solution was a masterpiece of civic single-mindedness and determination, coupled with Texas ingenuity and legal sleight-of-hand.

The amount of cash urgently needed to purchase the optioned land was estimated to be $500,000, based on an average price of $230 per acre. The city's leaders, finally accepting the fact that the U.S. government really did not intend to provide the necessary funds, swung into action. The chamber's military affairs committee established an entity known as the San Antonio Airport Company to raise sufficient money from local sources to purchase the 2,300-acre site. After one week, only $100,000 had been raised, and it was growing increasingly apparent that another funding source needed to be found and very quickly.

As the municipal government of San Antonio was also clearly in a position to benefit economically from a new military airfield, and just as certainly liable to suffer from the loss of Kelly and Brooks, the chamber logically enough petitioned the city council for its financial support. Unfortunately, the city did not have a spare half-million dollars in its budget. Further, the city attorney had determined that even if the city could find such an amount of available cash, it could not legally use public funds to acquire land that was to be donated to the federal government for any purpose whatsoever.[15]

With time growing short and the prospect of a financial calamity looming ever larger, the chamber desperately sought a second opinion on the city attorney's ruling. In a last minute appeal, chamber executives convinced a local judge, James Sluder, to rule that the city could in fact issue interest bearing notes for what could be rather loosely termed "unspecified municipal purposes."[16]

The city council, apparently easily satisfied with the correctness of Judge Sluder's opinion that reversed the ruling of its own city attorney, blithely issued $500,000 in city notes ostensibly to fund the conveniently unspecified municipal purposes, while in reality the money raised was specifically to be used to buy the site for the new airfield. Even more intriguing was the fact that the notes were backed by some $5 million in apparently uncollectible back taxes long past due from delinquent tax payers. Just why the city council suddenly became optimistic that the taxes could almost miraculously be collected is not known. At any rate, both the

United States district attorney and the Texas attorney general promptly concurred that the San Antonio Airport Company could indeed borrow the necessary $500,000 from local banks to buy the land. It could then present the land to the city which would pay off the company's notes to the banks with the funds it would somehow manage to raise by collecting the back taxes. The city could then transfer title to the land to the federal government so that the new airfield could be built. Although it was convoluted and highly imaginative, the jerryrigged scheme worked.[17]

All on one momentous day, June 8, 1928, the banks loaned the required amount of $546,460 to the San Antonio Airport Company, the company paid the farmers the full amount due to them in cash, and the city then presented the hastily negotiated deeds to the United States of America. The company then passed the total debt back to the city council, which retired the full amount of the bank notes with back taxes that somehow had been collected after all. San Antonio had lived up to its part of the agreement with the Air Corps, albeit a bit curiously, and now it was up to the army to complete the pact.[18]

While the city had been struggling to locate and acquire an acceptable site for the new airfield, a young pilot serving as a dispatch officer at Kelly Field had been doodling on the back of his official worksheets. Learning of the plans to construct a new flying field, Lt. Harold Clark had begun sketching designs for what he thought might be an ideal air city. Clark had trained for a time as an architect prior to joining the service, and his military experience had convinced him that most existing airfields, including Kelly itself, were poorly designed for what were clearly the changing needs of aviation.

Clark's plan for his utopian airfield of the future consisted of a wheel-like layout, with streets radiating concentrically from a central hub. Within the wheel's 475-acre circle would be all the ground elements essential to an airfield. Administration offices, barracks, commissaries, and recreational facilities would in this way all be provided for within Clark's wheel. On three sides of the wheel, hangars and taxiways would be created, and on the east and west arcs of the wheel beyond the taxiways, there would be two runways. The overall design was a simple circle inside a square. The brash young lieutenant was thoroughly convinced that his revolutionary idea was viable and doubtless to his great surprise and delight, Gen. Frank Lahm agreed with him.[19]

The general, overseer of the entire project, arranged to have Clark immediately transferred to his staff on special assignment to further develop his plans. Though ultimately expanded and finely tuned by San Antonio's famed architectural firm of Ayers and Ayers, much of Lieutenant Clark's original layout for his futuristic air city became a reality at what soon became Randolph Field. A history of the base notes that Clark's "overall plan was so well designed, that notwithstanding all the tremendous advances in aviation, few changes have been necessary."[20] Harold Clark, who rose through the grades to become a brigadier general, rather ruefully admitted in later years that his design was by no means perfect in every respect, particularly the radiating and concentric roadway pattern. Late in his life, Clark told a Randolph historian, "I love this place, you know, but every time I come out here, I get lost."[21]

With a site secured and a working design in place, a committee of army aviators was appointed by General Lahm to select an appropriate name for the airfield soon to be constructed. One of the members of that committee was native Texan and veteran pilot Capt. William M. Randolph. On February 16, 1928, while on what had been planned as a routine flight, Captain Randolph was killed when his plane crashed at Gorman, Texas. Without hesitation, his fellow committeemen chose his name to be forever identified with the new field.

The U.S. Army Corps of Engineers estimated that the construction costs for the initial phase of the newly named Randolph Field would be $10 million. This projection proved to be remarkably accurate when the final expense report showed costs to have been just under $11 million in total. Based on the originally projected cost estimate, Randolph Field was expected to be the engineers' second largest project ever, only slightly less ambitious than the building of the Panama Canal. Because Lieutenant Clark's plan for the layout of the airfield was completed long before the actual site was selected, it was estimated that well over a year in construction time was saved and building costs reduced accordingly.

Clark's revolutionary design was difficult for some elements of the army's hidebound hierarchy to accept. The quartermaster general, Maj. Gen. C. F. Cheatham, felt strongly that it was within his command's authority to design the field, while Air Corps chief, Maj. Gen. James F. Fechet, liked the Clark plan mainly because it had been created by an army pilot who had personally observed the flaws in other military airfield layouts. The matter was finally resolved by Secretary of War Dwight Davis who, after hearing heated arguments in his office on October 17, 1928, concluded that "the quartermaster general would build Randolph the way the Air Corps wants it built." The Air Corps rightly viewed this as an historic occasion. For the first time, it had gotten its way in a very practical sense.[22]

The first commanding officer of the base, while it was still under construction, was Capt. Earl H. De Ford, who wrote in his log that all he saw upon his arrival were "a few construction shacks, a flagpole with a flag flying from it, and a Chinese restaurant."[23] The captain did not note if the restaurant had existed before government construction had started, or if it had been opened solely for the dining pleasure of the hundreds of working men who swarmed over the gigantic building site.

As construction activity progressed under Captain De Ford's watchful eye, Randolph Field's most distinctive architectural landmark began to take shape. At the center of Lieutenant Clark's hub was to be an administration building, complete with a water tower and a tall radio antenna. Safety conscious flyers, however, pointed out the desirability of limiting the number of vertical protrusions to a bare minimum, motivating the on-site project planners to seek a way to consolidate the required vertical elements into one structure. The result was the famous "Taj Mahal" tower, the enduring trademark of Randolph Field. Costing $252,027.50 and standing over 170 feet in height, the "Taj" that would eventually loom above the administration building was actually a resplendent shell disguising both a 500,000 gallon water tower and the radio mast. Attesting to both its beauty and its function, the building was placed on the National Registry of Historic Places in 1987.[24]

In 1930, as construction on the base neared the halfway completion point, it was decided to stage a rather elaborate if somewhat premature dedication ceremony. On June 30 of that year, with construction continuing on every acre of the huge and inconveniently rain-soaked site, the ceremonies commenced.

Approximately 15,000 to 20,000 people gathered in a muddy

field to hear dedicatory addresses by Texas Governor Dan Moody, Gen. Frank Lahm, and other dignitaries. Just a few minutes before the governor was due to arrive by automobile from Austin, however, sharp-eyed observers in the throng noticed smoke pouring from an approaching black vehicle. Later, witnesses were unable to agree if the automobile had been a Lincoln or a Cadillac, as their eyes were apparently not quite sharp enough to discern the difference at that distance. At any rate, all spectators did concur that they could see the limousine's passengers begin to leave the car hurriedly as the smoke began billowing forth from it in great clouds. Their unseemly haste proved to be fortuitous when the vehicle, be it Cadillac or Lincoln, suddenly exploded.[25]

As the erstwhile occupants of the now blazing car slogged their way toward the flag-bedecked speakers' platform, army officers dispatched a tow truck to fetch what had only minutes before been the governor's official limousine. Much to the delight of the assembled crowd, the truck promptly slid into an all but bottomless mud hole and virtually disappeared from sight.

A game Governor Moody, a bit mudspattered but obviously undaunted, at last reached the speakers' platform, whereupon a firing squad dutifully discharged the obligatory seventeen-gun salute in his honor. The *San Antonio Light*, in reporting the day's events, failed to mention how the roar of the army's guns compared with the noise made by the governor's car as it exploded on the muddy road from Austin.

Despite his earlier misadventure, Governor Moody delivered what proved to be a singularly prophetic address:

> "It occurs to me," said the governor, "that the future of our whole country may depend on a well-trained Air Corps. All that we are to become may depend on the men who are trained on this field. . . . It may be that we must depend upon the heroes of the air for the defense of the future."[26]

After giving a short response to the governor's uncannily prescient remarks, General Lahm assisted the widow of Captain Randolph in raising the first United States flag to officially fly over the field that was destined to forever bear the name of her late husband. Among the witnesses to this moving event was Captain Randolph's sister, Ellen. She had traveled to the ceremonies from

March Field in California as a passenger in an army aircraft. In so doing, she became the first woman ever to fly in an Air Corps plane, at least officially. The aircraft in which she was the passenger was piloted by Maj. Millard F. Harmon, Jr., who rose to the rank of four star general in World War II.[27]

In addition to the governor's exploding limousine incident, another highlight of Randolph Field's dedication ceremony was an aerial exhibition staged by 233 aircraft gathered in San Antonio for the event. In her 1931 notes on the day's activities, Ellen Randolph wrote that the air parade, billed as the largest such formation ever staged, "brought gasps of amazement from the spectators." Far more than a simple fly-by of aeroplanes, the demonstration included simulated air-to-air combat, the strafing of balloons by pursuit planes, and a massed "dropping of men and machine guns by parachute." Miss Randolph concluded her essay by noting that the entire maneuver was "carried out in perfect precision [even though the] landing gear of some of the planes was less than 50 ft. from the ground."[28] It had already been quite a day, but there was more to come.

The dedicatory celebration concluded with a gala city-sponsored banquet at San Antonio's Gunter Hotel. A telegram from President Herbert Hoover was read, his words extolling the successful joint civilian and military effort that had brought the new base into at least partial existence. In what was perhaps a sly reference to the city's initial snail-like progress in donating the land to the government, the president lauded "the patriotic spirit of your citizens in presenting this field to the Government."[29] As *The San Antonio Express* trumpeted, "This is our night. Our city will forever be in the forefront of military aviation, and all San Antonio should rejoice in that confidence."[30]

Following the brief celebration, work on Randolph continued at a steady pace. By November 1931, enough of the facility was completed to permit the introduction of the first class of cadets to their new classrooms and runways. The official transfer of the headquarters of both the Air Corps Basic Flying School from Brooks Field and the Primary Training School from March Field to Randolph occurred in late October.

As the newly established center for both primary and basic training, Randolph's mission was to prepare flying cadets for the final advance instruction they would obtain at San Antonio's other big base, Kelly Field. In the primary phase of training, the neophyte flyer attended ground school, endured strenuous physical training, and learned the fundamentals of military life. One former cadet remembered that for the first two weeks his class was on the field, they did "nothing but close order drill for fifty minutes out of every hour, with a ten minute rest period, for ten hours a day."[31] In a few months, the cadets received enough ground school and flying training to pilot the PT-3 aircraft without an instructor on board.

After soloing and logging at least sixty-five hours in the air, the Randolph cadets went on to the basic training school on the field. In this phase of their development as pilots, they were introduced to faster aircraft and the mysteries of aerial navigation. Night flying and solo cross-country flights rounded out the curriculum.

The life of a cadet in the primary school was made somewhat more difficult by the hazing that was then prevalent in America's armed forces. All primary cadets, known as "Dodos," were required to wear their flying goggles at breakfast in the cadet mess hall and to emulate an airplane in a banking configuration as they turned a corner, with arms outstretched while dog-trotting about the field. Each time a cadet passed a mailbox, he was required to halt, salute it, and bow low before trotting off to his destination. Fortunately, the cadet's tour in primary school was blessedly short and the total period of the combined primary and basic instruction was eight months. One cadet, however, recalled his long summer months at Randolph as consisting of a seemingly endless succession of the longest and hottest days of his life.[32]

Successful cadets from Randolph then proceeded across the city to Kelly Field's advanced training course. The original plan to include advanced training along with the primary and basic phases at Randolph was abandoned when air traffic proved to be far too congested. At Kelly the students learned to use an airplane as a weapon and began to specialize as pilots of either pursuit, bomber, or transport-type aircraft. Upon completing this final phase of their training, the cadets were presented with their aviators wings, the gold bars of a second lieutenant, and received their orders placing them on active duty at a salary of $205 per month. They were each successful products of what was commonly known as San Antonio's pilot-maker machine, having learned their aeronautical skills not fifteen miles from where Benny Foulois had brought his single plane squadron to San Antonio in 1910.

RANDOLPH FIELD GOES TO WAR

It was pretty obvious to all of us that America would have to get in the war sooner or later. For most of us cadets, sooner sounded a lot better than later.

G. William Borland
San Antonio, Texas
August 1998

By 1939, with the war in Europe escalating hourly, the army's flight training program accelerated. The air service's annual pilot production goal was more than doubled to 7,000 pilots per year. Within months, the goal was raised again to 12,000 and then shortly thereafter, the Air Corps announced it would be seeking 30,000 newly-minted pilots each year. In time, the theoretical goal for new pilots reached 93,000 annually.[33] The impact of this vastly increased demand for pilots was clearly bound to affect Randolph Field significantly. Between 1939 and 1941, the number of cadets reporting to the field grew by 250 percent, while the number of those successfully completing the primary and basic phases of training and going on to Kelly Field's advanced school increased by 375 percent.[34]

Although more and more cadets arrived at Randolph, the fundamental training regimen stayed essentially the same. The introduction of faster and more reliable aircraft constituted the only significant change in the way the U.S. Army Air Force taught its cadets to be pilots. The looming possibility that war was imminent injected a new level of urgency and seriousness into what had previously been routine peacetime training.

Even when war did come to the United States in late 1941, however, the life of an aviation cadet at Randolph Field was not all drilling, ground school, and learning to fly an airplane. In fact, there is much evidence that a cadet's social life in San Antonio was both active and pleasurable.

On the second Saturday following his arrival at Randolph, each cadet was invited to attend a tea-dance held in honor of the incoming class at the Flying Cadet Club located in the Gunter Hotel in downtown San Antonio. At this event, the upperclassmen would introduce the newcomers to many of the city's coterie of attractive young ladies. However, it would seem that little in the way of a formal introduction was necessary. The 1942 edition of the official guide given to each Randolph cadet upon his arrival stated unequivocally that:

> By virtue of his flying cadetship, the Randolph Field newcomer is recognized without further test as being personally and socially eligible, and during his stay in the San Antonio neighborhood, he will have no difficulty in securing reasonable dates.[35]

While no definition of the word "reasonable" was volunteered by the author of the guidebook, the implication was clear that a cadet could easily enjoy a successful social life in San Antonio if he so desired. In fact, the book went on to observe that "if a cadet does not have a date, it is usually his own fault."[36]

The Flying Cadet Club apparently was the center for the cadets' social activity in town long after the introductory tea-dance event. The rules of decorum were simple enough. There was to be no excessive drinking, no conspicuous dress, and curiously, no jitterbug dancing. To visit the club, most cadets were free to leave the base after dinner on Saturday and not required to return to it until 9:30 Sunday evening.[37]

On one Sunday afternoon in October 1942, the cadets arrived at the Gunter only to find the hotel swarming with aging but still garrulous members of the Old Trail Drivers Association. The grizzled former cowboys delighted in regaling the young airmen with tales of their colorful exploits along the Chisholm, Goodnight-Loving, and other legendary cattle trails. Judging by the picture of the event that appeared in *The San Antonio Light*, at least two of the cadets found the old-timers' accounts almost too colorful to accept on first hearing.[38]

The Gunter Hotel's official history notes that "[Randolph's] 'Flying Cadets' were celebrated as an elite corps. Cadets were treated with deference, even in entertainment." Each Sunday afternoon, much of the hotel's public space was reserved for the cadets, who danced with "select young ladies," and dined from lavish buffets prepared by the Gunter's chefs. "All during the war," states the hotel's history booklet, "tea-dances at the Gunter were part of the social scene in San Antonio." While a few cadets with automobiles ventured the eighty miles to Austin and the social life surrounding the University of Texas in that city, most were content to go no farther than the Flying Cadet Club in downtown San Antonio.[39]

Some of the girls who frequented the club apparently acquired some reflected military training of their own. Cadets occasionally communicated with one another in code, smugly tapping out various observations about their dates who were seated with them at a club table. Much to the dismay and embarrassment of the cadets, they often discovered that many of the girls could read Morse Code nearly as well as they could. Fortunately, the unanticipated codebreaking did not seem to have been socially disastrous. As the Randolph Field Cadet Guidebook observed as early as 1942, "so many officers have married the local girls, San Antonio is called the 'Mother-in-law' of the Army."[40]

Even more officers were soon to arrive in the city. With the need for an ever increasing number of pilots, it became apparent early in the war that a great many more flight instructors would be required. Consequently, in 1943, Randolph's mission was expanded to include a flying school for those who would teach others to fly. For the next two years and until the end of the war, Randolph saw nearly 13,000 pilot instructors successfully complete their training on the base.[41]

Although many other bases around the state turned out highly capable pilots during the war, Randolph enjoyed a reputation as being perhaps a bit more elite than the rest, and well-deserving of its title as "The West Point of the Air." Indeed, when cadets at the U.S. Military Academy at West Point, New York, wished to learn to fly and to serve with the Army Air Force, they were transferred to Randolph Field. One training class, 42-K, was made up largely of former West Point cadets. To distinguish them from their classmates, this elite group wore black shoes instead of brown ones, along with black ties and a specially designed insignia. Among the transferred cadets from West Point was young B. D. Randolph, son of the man for whom the field had been named not quite fifteen years earlier.[42]

In all, Randolph Field trained over 16,000 pilots in World War II in addition to the instructor pilots. Cadets had come to the base from other countries as well, with six arriving from Brazil, three from Mexico and nearly twenty from other Latin American countries. San Antonio's great air training center had become international in scope.[43]

The arrival of the cadets from all across the United States and from foreign countries meant big business for San Antonio. Officers and their families along with the many civilian employees assigned to the city's base caused the population to swell. During the war years, San Antonio's population soared by 61 percent. Even in a sometimes restrictive wartime economy, business in the city was in nearly all respects better than it had ever been.[44]

Clearly, the decision of San Antonio's civic leaders to pursue the acquisition of what was to become Randolph Field had been a sound one. The millions of dollars that had been pumped into a depression-ravaged economy by the construction work on the field in the early 1930s had allowed the city to weather that storm. Moreover, the war-generated population and business boom of the 1940s had given San Antonio a powerful boost from which it would benefit well into the future.

POSTWAR ADJUSTMENTS

Alamo City To Continue As Air Leader

Headline
The San Antonio Light
November 8, 1945

Unlike many smaller Texas cities, San Antonio did not suffer from radical military realignments following the end of World War II. To be sure, fewer numbers of pilot and flight crew trainees entered the gates at Randolph Field after the war, but there were no initial economically catastrophic base closures such as those experienced by Sweetwater, Pecos, Pyote, Harlingen, and many other Texas towns.

For a time following the war, Randolph Air Force Base continued to train pilots, but with the advent of the Korean War in 1950, the instructional emphasis switched to crew training. The last class of cadet pilots left the base in late August 1951. In the early years of the Cold War, Randolph continued to offer instruction to crews of many of the U.S. Air Force's leading operational aircraft including the B-29, the B-50, the B-57, and the KC-97.

In more recent years, the base has fulfilled many changing training missions to meet the needs of the nation. In 1996, it became the first school to jointly train navigator candidates for both the air force and the navy. The 12th Flying Training Wing also continued the base's long standing tradition of producing pilot instructors. In all, over 90,000 airmen, pilots and navigators alike, have undergone training at Randolph since its founding in 1931.[45]

Gen. Frank Lahm, "The Father of Randolph Field," would find many reasons to be proud of his pet project. The base now sprawls across 5,237 acres and boasts a military population of over 5,000. There are 4,300 civilian employees on the facility, and the combined military and civilian annual payroll is close to $400 million. The overall U.S. Air Force payroll for its bases in San Antonio exceeded $1 billion in 1997. Further, many of the men and women who were stationed at Randolph over the years have chosen to return to the Alamo City upon leaving the air force. Their fond memories of warm South Texas hospitality and the legendary mild climate of the region have been sufficient to lure them back to the city. The impact of the annual expenditures of thousands of military retirees on the community's economy is enormous. Clearly, San Antonio's $546,460 investment in military aviation nearly seventy years ago has paid handsome dividends each and every year since.[46]

Maybe little Benny Foulois somehow knew it was all going to happen. Perhaps he sensed that his faith in military aviation would be proved valid, along with his conviction that San Antonio would play a significant and lasting role in the evolution of flight. At a farewell banquet given in his honor on July 7, 1911, the departing lieutenant told his listeners that although he had been the only military aviator in San Antonio and even though he and the army's only aeroplane were heading east the next day, he was confident that someday another aviator with yet another aeroplane would come to take his place. That his modest prediction would in fact come to pass to such an astounding degree might well have surprised even the bantam flyer, whose farsightedness and perseverance had done so much to launch San Antonio on its long and successful career as America's premier military capital city of the air.

A 1958 photograph of the widely publicized and still controversial sign that greeted visitors to Greenville for nearly fifty years.

— Copyright©, Photography by Narramore
Greenville, Texas. Used by permission

Construction begins with clearing and grading work on Majors Army Airfield, August 1942.
— Courtesy, 12th Flying Training Wing Historian Office, Randolph AFB, Texas

An aerial view shows work on the nearly completed Majors Field in December 1942.
— Courtesy, 12th Flying Training Wing Historian Office, Randolph AFB, Texas

Republic P-47s in flight over East Texas.
— Courtesy, 12th Flying Training Wing Historian Office,
Randolph AFB, Texas

A rare photograph of the 201st Mexican Fighter Squadron that was taken shortly after its arrival in Texas in August 1944.
— Courtesy, Air Education Training Command History Office, Randolph AFB, Texas

The airfield's legacy: a part of Raytheon Corporation's huge Greenville operation at Majors Field as it appeared in 1998.
— Author's Photograph

A sign at the entrance to Greenville's Municipal Airport honors the World War II base that once flourished nearby.
— Author's Photograph

MAJORS ARMY AIRFIELD

IN 1941 THE CIVIL AERONAUTICS ADMINISTRATION (CAA)
INFORMED GREENVILLE OFFICIALS THAT THE CITY WOULD
RECEIVE FEDERAL ASSISTANCE TO BUILD A CIVILIAN AIRPORT
AS PART OF THE COUNTRY'S PREPARATION FOR POSSIBLE
ENTRY INTO WORLD WAR II. IN APRIL 1941 U.S. CONGRESSMAN
SAM RAYBURN NOTIFIED HUNT COUNTY THAT THE CIVILIAN
AIRPORT PROJECT WOULD BECOME PART OF A $5 MILLION
ARMY AIR FORCE TRAINING BASE HOUSING 3,000 TO 4,000
PERSONNEL AND 300 AIRPLANES. THE BASE WAS NAMED FOR
LT. TRUETT MAJORS, THE FIRST PILOT FROM HUNT COUNTY
KILLED IN ACTION IN WORLD WAR II.

CONSTRUCTION OF THE BASE AND THREE AUXILIARY AIRFIELDS
IN THE COUNTY BOOSTED THE LOCAL ECONOMY AND PROVIDED
EMPLOYMENT FOR THOUSANDS OF AREA RESIDENTS. THE BASE
BECAME FULLY OPERATIONAL ON JANUARY 5, 1943.

MAJORS ARMY AIRFIELD PROVIDED CADET PILOTS WITH
PREFLIGHT AND PRIMARY TRAINING. WHEN NOT EXERCISING,
STUDYING, OR TRAINING IN BT-13s AND P-47s THE CADETS
VISITED GREENVILLE FOR RECREATION AND TO SOCIALIZE
WITH LOCAL CITIZENS. IN ADDITION TO U.S. ARMY AIR CORPS
PILOTS, COMPANIES OF WOMEN'S ARMY CORPS MEMBERS, ROYAL
AIR FORCE PILOTS, AND MEXICAN AIR FORCE PILOTS WERE
TRAINED HERE. THE BASE BECAME AN ADVANCED TRAINING
CENTER BEFORE BEING DEACTIVATED ON JULY 15, 1945.
SESQUICENTENNIAL OF TEXAS STATEHOOD 1845-1995

*A Texas Historical Commission Marker salutes the old airfield indicating
where the base was and why it was important. This is an all too rare sight
throughout the state.*

— Author's Photograph

Early wartime security was tight at Waco Field's main gate.
— Courtesy, Richard J. Veit, Waco, Texas

*John T. Sprague,
Waco's first
commander,
remained in
command throughout
the war years . . .
and beyond.*
— Courtesy, Richard J.
Veit, Waco, Texas

The first training flight is ready for takeoff from Waco Army Airfield.
— Courtesy, Richard J. Veit, Waco, Texas

Aviation Cadet Mitchell gets some pre-flight pointers from his instructor.
— Courtesy, Richard J. Veit, Waco, Texas

BT-13s on the ramp at Waco Army Airfield early in the war.
— U.S. Air Force Photo.
— Courtesy of the University of Texas Institute of Texan Cultures at San Antonio.
Used by permission.

*Lt. Col. John T.
Sprague became a full
colonel after a short
time at Waco.*
— Courtesy, Richard J.
Veit, Waco, Texas

All newly arrived cadets were invited to a tea-dance at Waco's Shrine Club.
— Courtesy, Richard J. Veit, Waco, Texas

*A truck provides chaperoned transportation back to Waco
after a party at the field.*
— Courtesy, Richard J. Veit, Waco, Texas

Social life at Waco Airfield was often the talk of the town.
— Courtesy, Richard J. Veit, Waco, Texas

Baylor University coeds greeted aviation cadets with patriotic enthusiasm.
— Courtesy, Richard J. Veit, Waco, Texas

*Civilians were always eager to
visit Waco Army Airfield.*
— Courtesy, Richard J. Veit,
Waco, Texas

In Waco This Is
"Bomber Week"
Buy Bonds to Buy a Bomber!

Here's your chance to help win the war.
Buy War Bonds now to buy a bomber car-
rying this name, "The City of Waco, Texas."
Buy to the limit of your capacity . . because
now's the time to put your money to work
for your country and for your own safety.
Buy Bonds to Buy a Bomber! War Bonds and
Stamps on sale here.

*Waco's first bond drive was
dedicated to buying a bomber.*
— Courtesy, Richard J. Veit, Waco, Texas

*After the successful bond drive, "The City of Waco, Texas" rolls off the line
at the Boeing Plant.*
— Courtesy, Richard J. Veit, Waco, Texas

*Waco school children collected over six tons of scrap metal
in their first drive.*
— Courtesy, Richard J. Veit, Waco, Texas

*Farmer Chapin's barn yielded more scrap than the school kids
found in their entire neighborhood.*
— Courtesy, Richard J. Veit, Waco, Texas

The "Waco Victory," freighter-
transport recently constructed, is
carrying men and supplies to the
far-flung battle fronts of global
war. It has been assigned to
American Mail Lines, Ltd., Seattle,
at request of a Waco girl, Miss
Elizabeth Finucane, an employe of
the company; and it is commanded
by one of the line's most noted
masters, Capt. E. J. Stull, who is
holder of the British distinguished
service cross. This cross was
awarded Captain Stull by King
George for his outstanding leader-
ship during the allied amphibious
attack on Sicily.

"The Waco Victory" saluted the city's dedication to the war effort.
— Courtesy, Richard J. Veit, Waco, Texas

*Baylor University's role in the war
earned it a namesake ship,
"The Baylor Victory."*
— Courtesy, Richard J. Veit, Waco, Texas

*The once bright red and white
water tower is one of the few visible
reminders of James Connally Air
Force Base and its predecessor.*
— Author's Photograph

Benjamin D. Foulois, Maj. Gen. USAF (Ret), father of military aviation in Texas and ironically the principal speaker at the final graduation ceremony at James Connally AFB. 1965.
— Courtesy, The University of Texas Barker Texas History Center.
Used by permission of the University of Texas Institute of Texan Cultures at San Antonio

Lt. Benjamin Foulois is pictured fifty-four years before he spoke at James Connally AFB. The picture was made at Fort Sam Houston, Texas, birthplace of San Antonio's reputation as the nation's capital of military aviation.
— Courtesy, The University of Texas Barker Texas History Center. Used by permission of the University of Texas Institute of Texan Cultures at San Antonio

Gen. Frank P. Lahm was the "Father of Randolph Field"
and a shrewd negotiator.
— Used by permission of the University of Texas
Institute of Texan Cultures at San Antonio

Awaiting demolition is one of the German homesteads acquired in 1928
to build Randolph Field.
— The *San Antonio Express-News* Collection
Used by permission of the University of Texas
Institute of Texan Cultures at San Antonio

*Capt. William M. Randolph,
for whom Randolph Field was
named, was a member of the
commission appointed to
choose a name for the base. He
was killed in a plane crash.*
—— Courtesy, The *San Antonio
Express-News* Collection
Used by permission of the University
of Texas Institute of Texan Cultures
at San Antonio

*Lt. Harold D. Clark was the
pilot and novice architect who
designed Randolph Field while
serving as a motor pool officer.*
— Courtesy, 12th Flying Training
Wing Historian Office,
Randolph AFB, Texas

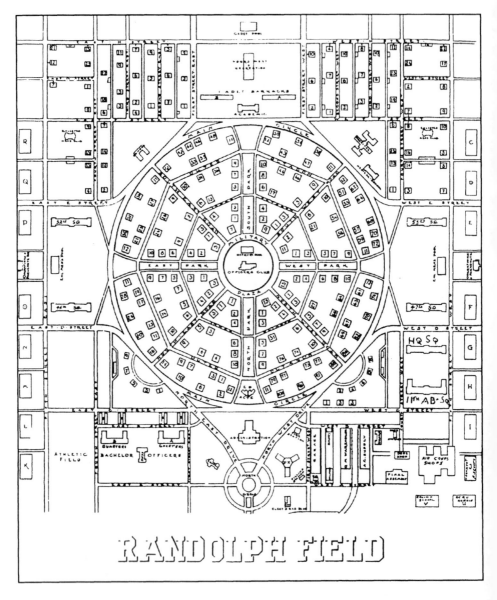

RANDOLPH FIELD

Lt. Clark's original layout for Randolph Field was first sketched on the back of a dispatch sheet.
— Courtesy, Air Education and Training Command History Office, Randolph AFB, Texas

*Randolph Field is shown as a work in progress in 1934 and
photographed from 8,000 feet.*
— Courtesy, 12th Flying Training Wing Historian Office,
Randolph AFB, Texas

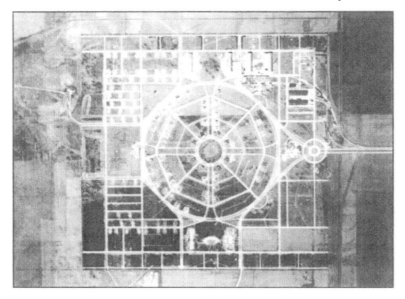

*The field from directly overhead showing construction work on buildings
and runways, just as Clark envisioned it. 1934.*
— Courtesy, Air Education and Training Command History Office,
Randolph AFB, Texas

Ellen Randolph, sister of Capt. William Randolph, departs March Field to attend the dedication ceremony at Randolph Field in June 1930. She was the first female to fly in a military aircraft. The plane was piloted by Maj. Millard F. Harmon who became a four-star general during World War II.
— Courtesy, 12th Flying Training Wing Historian Office, Randolph AFB, Texas

Texas Governor Dan Moody, none the worse for wear following an exploding limousine incident, addresses the crowd at the dedication ceremony at Randolph. June 1930.
— The *San Antonio Express-News* Collection. Used by permission of the University of Texas Institute of Texan Cultures at San Antonio

One year following the dedication ceremony, Randolph's "Taj Mahal" was nearing completion. Hidden within the elaborate tower are a water tank and a radio mast. July 1931.
— Courtesy of Florence Collett Ayres. Used by permission of the University of Texas Institute of Texan Cultures at San Antonio

Still in their civilian finery, cadet candidates arrive at the "Taj Mahal" for processing early in World War II.
— Courtesy, 12th Flying Training Wing Historian Office, Randolph AFB, Texas

Somewhat skeptically, cadets mingle with Texas cattlemen at the Old Trail Drivers convention held at the Gunter Hotel in October 1942. The newspaper caption identified the ranchers as L. C. Kaufman and H. O. Campbell. The cadets are John B. Modica of New Jersey and Don Jones from Albany, New York.
— The *San Antonio Light* Collection. Used by permission of the University of Texas Institute of Texan Cultures at San Antonio

Harold D. Clark, Brigadier General USAF [Ret], designer of Randolph Field, stands in front of his Taj Mahal. As a visitor to the base, the general confessed he often got lost in the roadway maze he had designed.
— Courtesy, 12th Flying Training Wing Historian Office, Randolph AFB, Texas

*A rousing view of Randolph Field's landmark Taj Mahal in all of its grandeur.
Note that the "USA" formation-keeping aircraft are biplanes.*
—The *San Antonio Express-News* Collection. Used by permission of the
University of Texas Institute of Texan Cultures at San Antonio

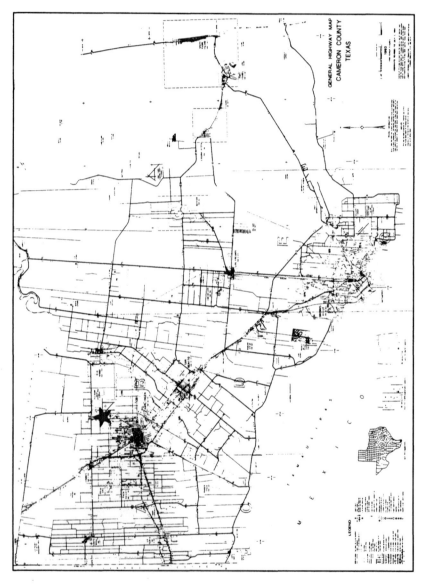

Cameron County Map. This map of western Cameron County shows the location of Harlingen Army Airfield during the war years. An inset map of Texas shows the location of the county within the state.

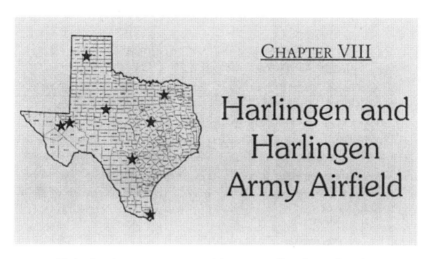

Chapter VIII

Harlingen and Harlingen Army Airfield

All the land I've seen around here is so flat that when it commences to rain, the water's got no place to run off to, so the flowers grow wild and pretty. If old Cap would only let us slow down a tad, I would surely like to rest here for a spell.

Pvt. Enos W. Murfin
"A Texas Volunteer" June 1846
Quoted in the *Brownsville Herald*
Sesquicentennial Issue
January 1, 1986

Pvt. E. W. Murfin and his unidentified but clearly hard-driving captain were among the many soldiers who marched from San Antonio in 1846 to join Gen. Zachary Taylor on the banks of the Rio Grande. On their way south to fight in what would become known as the Mexican War, their rapid line of march took them within a few miles of the future site of Harlingen, Texas.

The country through which Taylor's soldiers so hastily marched was semi-tropical with a lush landscape of thick grasses and the colorful flowers that had earned the admiration of Enos Murfin. Cool breezes from the nearby Gulf of Mexico usually made the hot afternoon sun feel at least somewhat less tropical in its intensity. Only the nearness of the Rio Grande and the prospect of perhaps soon being shot at by a Mexican *soldado* could have cast a shadow over the American soldiers' impressions of what much later would be known as "The Magic Valley."

For nearly half a century following the Mexican War, the Lower Rio Grande Valley, magic or not, remained very much as the soldiers had first viewed it in 1846. Some of them had stayed in the area following the war, operating steamships on the river and engaging in lucrative trade with their former enemies. Many post-war newcomers passed through the Valley, following the river's trail on their way to the California gold fields during the rush of 1849. Bandits preyed upon the would-be prospectors, making the journey across the mostly unpopulated region a risky venture. Violence and lawlessness were everyday occurrences in what had become Cameron County, established in 1848 immediately follow-ing the war south of the Rio Grande.

The coming of America's Civil War in 1861 brought great activity to Cameron County as well as to the nearby Mexican sea-ports located on the Gulf Coast. European ships arrived in the lit-tle ports on a regular basis, their holds bulging with Confederate war supplies to be exchanged for the Southern-grown cotton that was in such short supply in England and on the Continent. Each bale loaded on board the ships sailing back to Europe carried an official-looking stamp that identified it as "Mexican Cotton." Fear-ing unwanted international repercussions, the captains of the pa-trolling Union blockade gunboats usually chose not to challenge the origin of the cotton cargo, and the effect of the blockade on the waters of the southern Gulf of Mexico was largely nullified. Vast fortunes were made, however, by many of those individuals who were engaged in bringing ships through what proved to be one of the widest breaches in the United States Navy's cordon around the maritime states of the Confederacy.

In the years following the Civil War, railroads replaced steam-ships as the principal mode of transportation in the Lower Rio Grande Valley. This practical and popular improvement made pos-sible a rapidly emerging agricultural economy that would soon prove to be of incalculable value to the entire region. Principal among the commercial crops were the citrus products that eventu-ally brought both wealth and worldwide fame to the Valley.

In 1904, some twenty miles north of General Taylor's old Fort Brown on the Rio Grande and alongside the military road that some of his soldiers had taken to reach it, developer Lon C. Hill founded the town of Harlingen. For some now obscure reason, he saw fit to give his new city a name borrowed from a town in far off Holland. The Texas version of Harlingen grew slowly but surely enough, its population reaching 1,126 in 1910 and 1,748 ten years later. Through the efforts of pioneering developers such as Hill and his associates, what had previously been a wild, brush covered land was soon transformed into a garden spot with irrigation canals replacing brackish swamps and citrus groves taking over where only cactus and mesquite had once flourished.[1]

Although much had changed in far South Texas since Private Murfin had passed through it in 1846, even greater elements of change were on the way to Harlingen in the middle of the twentieth century. A war that was taking place far away would in time prove to be pivotal to the city and to all of the Magic Valley.

HARLINGEN AERIAL GUNNERY SCHOOL

The terrain around Harlingen is totally unsuitable for organized military activity of any kind. There are no hills for suitable maneuvers by the cavalry and it is much too marshy for the infantry to march over.

Col. Edmund A. Pearce
Quoted in the
Valley Morning Star,
April 12, 1938

Col. Ed Pearce was clearly an officer of the old school. His shortsighted reasons for rejecting Harlingen as the site for any traditional organized military activity actually tended to make it a highly desirable location for an army airfield. Not only was the terrain flat, as the colonel had so astutely observed, it was also to a large degree devoid of any tall trees that might interfere with flight. Perhaps of even greater importance to airminded army officers than the terrain was the legendary climate of the Magic Valley, where the sun shone some 340 days a year, and where the temperature had dropped below freezing only three times in the twenty-nine years that such records had been kept. The average winter daytime temperature was shown to be 62° while the summertime thermometer readings seldom exceeded 84°.[2]

In 1938, perhaps stung by Colonel Pearce's dismissal of their city as a site for an infantry or cavalry installation, Harlingen's leaders began an aggressive campaign to have CAA inspectors survey the area as a possible site for a major airport that would benefit equally from the obviously suitable climate and terrain. In June 1940, Mayor Hugh Ramsey and chamber of commerce manager, Harvey Ratliff, succeeded in persuading the CAA that Harlingen would be an ideal place for the government to build one of the many airports it was creating. To attract the interest of the CAA, Mayor Ramsey had boldly approved the taking of an option on a nearly 1,000-acre site on the north edge of town as a potential location for such an airport. As an added incentive, the far-sighted mayor had also arranged for an additional 60,000 acres to be made available on the nearby King Ranch should the army later select the Harlingen facility as a military airfield.[3]

Although the CAA and the War Department were reported to be impressed with the sheer magnitude of Harlingen's land offer, they were characteristically secretive in making final arrangements for the proposed air installation. It was not until early 1941 that the citizens of the Valley first learned that any real progress had been made toward having a military base at Harlingen.

Early in the year without any advance notice to the city, the army abruptly advised the Texas Gamefish and Oyster Commission that nearby Padre Island was henceforth going to be used as a practice gunnery range, and that the aircraft that would be doing the shooting would be flying from an airfield that was to be constructed at Harlingen in the very near future. The immediate reaction to the army's curiously offhanded public announcement was understandably mixed. To the area's commercial fishermen who had long worked the seas off Padre Island for their livelihood, the news was devastating and prompted them to mount a serious protest to government officials. To Harlingen's townspeople, who learned of the army's intentions to build an airfield only through an article in the February 1, 1941, edition of the *Valley Morning Star,* the good news that the hard work of the mayor and the chamber of commerce had been successful was cause enough to stage a festive celebration.[4]

It took the army almost a full month to officially announce that the base had indeed been approved and that nearly $4 million had been budgeted for construction work on the facility. On May 31, 1941, the city of Harlingen's officials eagerly signed an agreement to rent the optioned land to the federal government for one dollar a year for twenty-four years with such terms to be renewable upon expiration of the rental contract. The city also gave the army the option of buying the land outright at any time at a fixed purchase price of $75 per acre for the nearly 1,000-acre tract.[5]

The U.S. Army Corps of Engineers moved swiftly to convert the farmland acreage into a functioning airfield which was slated to become a training facility for aerial gunners. A contractor's shack was erected on the property within six weeks of the signing of the lease and by September 1941, the 1,900 men laboring on the project had completed over 30 percent of the construction work. By mid-October, over half of the field was finished with all runways and streets in place, and work was completed on a chapel, a hospital, several barracks, and the headquarters building.[6]

Prior to its opening and during its first year of operations, the new facility was known as Harlingen Aerial Gunnery School, which was clearly an appropriate label. However, the resulting acronym HAGS touched off more than a few unfortunate attempts at humor and caused considerable embarrassment to the women soldiers assigned to the base. In June 1943, the name was obligingly changed to Harlingen Army Airfield.[7]

On November 28, 1941, while it was still officially known as HAGS, the base's first commanding officer, Col. John R. Morgan, made the initial landing on the newly constructed runway, bringing his PT-13 to a rolling stop directly in front of the looming control tower that was under construction. Nine days later, the United States was officially at war, first with Japan and then Germany and Italy. The very next day, Harlingen Aerial Gunnery School instructors began to teach men how to effectively use the deadly machine guns they would soon be firing from the turrets of big bombers at the Stukas and Zeros of the enemy. Before the students were permitted to even touch the machine guns, however, they perfected their aiming techniques with BB guns and then with shotguns on the skeet range.[8]

By Christmas Eve 1941, the residents of the Rio Grande Valley knew for certain that the new gunnery school was in operation. Bold face headlines in local newspapers advised readers to stay away from the coastal flats and lagunas along the Gulf Coast because gunnery students would be firing machine guns in the area all throughout the Christmas holidays and well into the new year. As one Harlingen newspaper put it, the Valley "was now a place where a warm Gulf breeze mixed powder smells with the scent of orange blossoms."[9]

The students at the Harlingen Aerial Gunnery School received six weeks of intensive instruction, three of which were devoted to familiarization, maintenance, and theory, with the balance of the course time spent on actual firing experience on the 46,000-acre range along the coast and in the air. The newly-developed Waller Trainer effectively simulated air-to-air combat conditions and helped ease the transition from ground firing to in-flight training. Once airborne, the gunnery trainees fired the .30 and .50 caliber machine guns first from the rear cockpits of AT-6 aircraft and then from the turrets of B-24, B-34, and B-37 bombers engaged in mock air battles at both high and low altitudes over the long barrier islands of the Gulf. The gunners' targets were rayon panels towed behind other aircraft which were occasionally flown by some of the WASP who were assigned to the school.[10]

Because their training schedule was so condensed, the students seldom had sufficient time or energy to travel even the short three miles into downtown Harlingen. During their six-week stay at the school, most students found time to go into town only once or twice. Even then, they were required to be back on the base by 11:00 P.M. on weeknights and 1:00 A.M. on the weekends. Other military personnel assigned to the base had no such stringent restrictions and they regularly trooped into town and frequently crossed the nearby Rio Grande to visit Matamoros, Mexico.

In 1943, Hollywood discovered Harlingen. Paramount Pictures dispatched director William Pine and popular actors Richard Arlen, Jimmy Lydon, and Chester Morris to the Valley airfield to film a motion picture to be appropriately entitled "Aerial Gunner." *New York Daily News* critic Kate Cameron noted in the paper's June 25, 1943, edition that the film was "packed with enough aerial action to satisfy any motion picture fan."[11] Another reviewer, however, found the script flawed with the film's chief asset being "the fact that most of it was shot on location at the U.S. Army Air Force Aerial Gunnery School at Harlingen, Texas."[12]

The cast and crew spent two weeks on the airfield with Arlen, as one of the stars, being filmed actually learning to fire the .30 caliber machine guns alongside true-to-life, and doubtlessly thrilled, army gunnery trainees. According to one report, the location shooting not only gave the film a decidedly un-Hollywood air of authenticity, it also helped substantially reduce the cost of production. On May 10, 1943, "Aerial Gunner" had its world premiere on the base, with military officers and studio officials in attendance. Several longtime residents of the city fondly recall the excitement and pride they felt when they first saw the film for themselves.

Some other old-timers remember when another Hollywood-inspired excitement gripped the Harlingen area during the war. When newspaper accounts confirmed reports that movie idol Clark Gable had enlisted in the army to become an aerial gunner, a rumor rapidly circulated that he was already on his way to Harlingen to learn his new wartime trade. The airfield's telephone switchboard was flooded by calls from local townspeople seeking to verify the rumor and to learn exactly when the movie star would be arriving. Despite repeated denials by senior officers, the rumor persisted until it was ultimately reported that Gable, who actually was a combat crew gunner, was already seeing action in the skies over Germany. As one now elderly lady recollects, "We were just so disappointed to find out he wasn't coming after all. Some girls swore they'd seen him driving out of the base, but I guess they were just day-dreaming."[13]

According to most existing accounts, the relationship between army personnel and the citizens of the Valley was an amicable one, except perhaps for some disillusionment when Clark Gable failed to make an appearance. Aside from the usual minor brushes with military police and civil authorities, no significant disturbances to the peace of Harlingen were permanently recorded.

Construction on the giant base was ongoing throughout the war years, with new barracks and improved training facilities being added regularly. According to many who were stationed at Harlingen during the war, the constantly expanding base was lush with tropical landscaping, which included many palm trees and two large citrus groves. The groves provided free although technically off-limits grapefruit and oranges to those soldiers brave enough to harvest them.

Lt. Col. John L. Kottal, who had served as an enlisted man at the airfield very early in the war, recalled many years later a system he had developed to share the forbidden fruit with his fellow airmen. When serving as a sentry, Kottal would pluck a grapefruit from a tree each time he passed a grove, giving it to the first sentry he met as he trudged along the field's perimeter. That sentry would then pass the fruit on to the first guard he would encounter and so on until Kottal's endless flow of grapefruit had ensured that each sentry walking the airfield's fence had received a grapefruit. "This was one of the ways in which we passed the time," Col. Kottal remembered, "and supplying each of the sentries on duty with at least one grapefruit usually took about eight hours."[14]

By February 1946, there was no longer a need for the citrus-eating sentries to walk their posts. Following the formal surrender of Japan in September 1945, it was announced that Harlingen Field was marked for closure. The obligatory protests against closing the multimillion-dollar facility were made by Harlingen's civic leaders to federal officials in Washington with the usual disappointing results. The base was soon completely abandoned, with its wartime mission of producing highly qualified aerial gunners successfully accomplished.

THE RETURN OF HARLINGEN FIELD

When I was stationed over in England in 1943 and on into 1944, I kept thinking about those palm trees and Gulf breezes back in Harlingen where I'd trained. At Mildenhall, any breezes that blew were like ice and most of the time I couldn't see any trees because of the mist and fog. I decided right there to get back to Texas just as soon as I could when the war was over.

Harlan F. Altman
San Benito, Texas
November 1998

At least statistically, the war years had been good for Harlingen. The population of the city had nearly trebled because of the airfield, and federally generated construction and payroll dollars had propelled the regional economy to previously undreamed of levels. Despite the eventual disappointment of the city's leaders over losing the giant base, the blow of its departure was at least somewhat softened by the postwar influx of many who had for a time served there during the conflict. Lured back to the Valley by their recollections of the almost perfect year around climate and the friendly reception they had previously enjoyed, hundreds of former gunners, their one-time instructors, and their pilots chose to make Harlingen their permanent home as soon as they became civilians again. The arrival of the veterans in the region soon after the war touched off both a land boom and feverish residential construction activity that were very material legacies of the closed airfield where they once had served.

With the beginning of the Korean War in June 1950, however, the dormant airfield took on a new life. Following a $17 million overhaul, the old airfield re-opened in June 1952 as Harlingen Air Force Base and a principal center for navigator training. Cadets and student officers alike trained at the school and by 1961, nearly 13,000 navigator-observers had graduated from it. Some 4,000 military personnel and over 700 civilians were permanently assigned to the base. Chamber of commerce estimates in 1960 indicated that the $25 million buying income generated by Harlingen AFB represented roughly half of all the money then being spent in the city. Receiving continued assurances from the Defense Department that such a vitally important base was to be a permanent air force installation, the city's leaders could only foresee continued growth and prosperity.[15]

As was often the case, their rose-tinted optimism came abruptly to an end in late 1961. To their dismay, Harlingen leaders received the completely unexpected announcement from Washington that the multimillion-dollar air base, which was even then still being expanded, was scheduled to be gradually phased out and then totally closed no later than June 30, 1962.

Almost at the same time as the shocking news from the Defense Department was received, the Valley's important citrus crop failed to materialize for the first time in decades. The twin financial disasters sent Harlingen and the entire Lower Rio Grande Valley into an economic free fall that would be felt for years. Real estate values plummeted as houses left vacant by suddenly departing air force personnel glutted the market. According to one long-time resident of the city, "It seemed like every other house on every block had either a for sale or a for rent sign on it."[16]

Soon, the once bustling air base was deserted and quiet. Weeds sprouted through cracks in the formerly active runways and only the outlines of concrete foundations served as reminders of the nearly five hundred buildings that had once stood on the base. Further, the unexpected and sudden death of Harlingen AFB had been particularly painful in terms of the relationship between the city and the federal government. Rather than transfer ownership of the land with all buildings intact to the city as had usually been the case in other base closures, the Defense Department had for some reason seen fit to merely auction the buildings to the highest bidders for removal or demolition for materials. The city was left with only the foundations or shells of the once useful structures. To make matters even worse, the federal government claimed that Harlingen owed it some $94,000 for an unrecovered investment cost incurred in sewer installations on the now abandoned base. In an effort to salvage something other than raw land from the base's closing, the city itself entered into the public auction and spent over $100,000 acquiring only a few of those derelict buildings that had not been snapped up by private bidders at garage sale prices.[17]

In time, the bitter differences between the city and the federal government were resolved and in July 1964, a full year after the base was completely closed, the title to the $18 million, 1,564-acre tract that had once been Harlingen Air Force Base was at last transferred to the city. It now owned what one newspaper account called "the most valuable white elephant in South Texas."[18]

Fortunately for the Valley, the city did not let their newly reacquired so-called white elephant remain idly at pasture for long. By 1970, the old base had been completely rebuilt or refurbished to emerge as the sleek new Rio Grande Valley International Airport, the only major commercial air terminal complex in the entire region. The air base jail was transformed into the attractive Rio Grande Valley Museum and the Marine Military Academy made impressive use of much of the old air force property. The TSTC system in time became something of a savior of dead air bases all across the state, and utilized much of the remaining space to provide sorely needed high quality technical training to the Valley.

In 1965, before plans for the future use of the old base were formulated, Harlingen Mayor Mike Hodes made a nearly classic whistle-past-the-graveyard comment. According to the mayor, "The closing of the Air Force base was the best thing that ever happened to us."[19] A chamber of commerce executive elaborated on the mayor's pronouncement by adding, "We've been forced to develop our own resources," and he concluded by saying, "I think you have to be in trouble before you get out and push."[20]

Harlingen was indeed in serious trouble when the base closed, but the entire city seems to have gotten out to push, creating a new sense of optimism for the future that the situation at the time did not seem to warrant. As evidence of its reawakened civic spirit, Harlingen was named one of America's ten most innovative and progressive cities in 1992, not quite thirty years after it had teetered on the edge of fiscal collapse. According to a local news source, "The comeback of the area once known as Harlingen Air Force Base has been a major factor in the city's economic success."[21]

The old World War II school for aerial gunners that became in time the air force's principal navigator training center did evolve as the crucial key to the economic success of Harlingen and the entire Magic Valley of the Rio Grande. Despite all of the growth and development, Private Murfin, who had marched through the region over 150 years before, might well be pleased to know that flowers still manage to bloom there, both brightly and in great abundance.

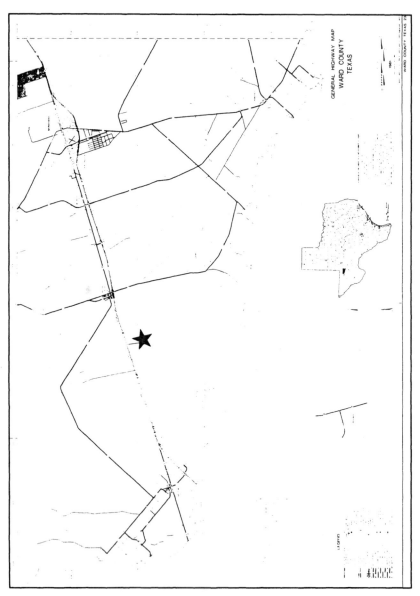

Ward County Map. This map of central Ward County shows the location of Pyote Army Airfield from 1941-1966. An inset map of Texas shows the location of the county within the state.

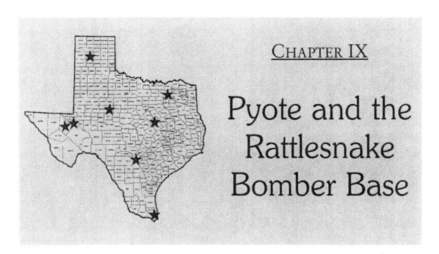

CHAPTER IX

Pyote and the Rattlesnake Bomber Base

I don't know why we even bothered to take that place away from them damned snakes. Since they liked it so much, I think we should have let them keep it all to themselves.

Art Pringle
Racine, Wisconsin
October 1998

As the Texas and Pacific Railway Company pushed its way westward in the early 1880s, it often established a telegraph station well in advance of the track-laying crews. One such station was placed in operation in far West Texas in June 1881 and given the colorful name of Pyote Tank. No one is certain just how the name came about. Some authorities believed it was derived from the railroad company's Chinese laborers' mispronunciation of the word "coyote," while a few of the local residents believe the town was named for the peyote cacti which is common to the region. In time, the word "tank" was dropped from the town's name.[1]

Pyote provides an interesting example of the boom and bust cycle that has historically plagued many Texas communities. Created by the railroad as it rolled westward on steel ribbons of newly laid track, the tiny community at first existed only to provide a stopping place for railway crews and laborers. By 1907, a post

office had been established and a general store was opened by
Cicero S. Sitton and his sons. To celebrate the opening of his new
emporium, Mr. Sitton invited all residents of Ward County to a barbecue, a social event that was so successful it lasted for three days.
Mr. Sitton took advantage of the festivities to circulate a petition
calling for a school to be established in the town, and shortly thereafter, Ward County's first schoolhouse opened in Pyote. Even with
a store and a school, the town grew slowly, reporting a population
of only one hundred people in 1925, fully forty-five years after the
opening of the railroad's advance station.[2]

The tiny community's fortunes soon changed, however, as oil
explorers moved into West Texas. In 1926, the giant Hendricks Oil
Field was discovered in Winkler County, located just thirty miles
from Pyote. The highly productive field, which would eventually
pump over six million barrels of sweet Texas crude each month,
instantly attracted the attention of virtually every major petroleum
exploration company. Probably much to the delight of Cicero Sitton and his successors, Pyote became almost overnight the bustling
center of oil activity for the entire region. Its Texas and Pacific railhead became the shipping point both for petroleum flowing out and
supplies and workers flooding into the oil field.[3]

Pyote had become a classic Texas oil boom town. Its population soared to over 3,500 and construction crews were hard pressed
to build houses, hotels, and stores rapidly enough to accommodate
the throngs of geologists and workers who were arriving daily. More
schools were built and new hard surfaced streets promptly replaced
the dirt roadways that had served the city since 1881. Pyote was
surely on its way to economic glory at last![4]

Suddenly, however, the boom was over. Just as swiftly as fortune had come to the town, misfortune arrived. The railroad built a
spur line directly from the Hendricks Oil Field to the nearby city
of Monahans, and abruptly there was no longer any reason to ship
men and material in or out of Pyote. By 1931, the town's population had dropped to just over 1,000 and by 1939, only two hundred
Texans called Pyote home. The classic pattern of economic boom
and bust had been all too painfully demonstrated.[5]

THE RATTLESNAKE BOMBER BASE

*Why anybody in his right mind wanted to build an air-
field out there, I'll never know. I thought it was a danged
fool notion then and I still think I was right.*

Harry G. Putnam
Midland, Texas
August 1998

According to the official book on Ward County history, the idea to build an army airfield at Pyote originated with County Commissioner Ted Thomas immediately following the attack on Pearl Harbor. The book relates that Commissioner Thomas went to the headquarters of the Army Corps of Engineers located in Roswell, New Mexico, to point out to the army men that the sun usually shone about 360 days a year in Pyote and that the land in the region was just about as flat as it was anywhere else on earth, there-fore making it an ideal site for an airfield.[6]

Although it is difficult to believe that the army's engineers were not aware of these less than startling facts about West Texas, it remains that either Commissioner Thomas or some other glib salesman convinced them that the idea for an airfield at Pyote was a sound one. After some prodding by Ward County officials, the University of Texas agreed to lease 2,745 acres of land it owned a mile west of the town to the federal government for the purpose of building an air base.

Official announcement of the new airfield was painfully slow in coming. The *Monahans News*, published at the county seat, could only offer rumors and unconfirmed reports to its readers who were, according to the newspaper, "waiting on edge" for the War Depart-ment to declare its intentions. News stories carried accounts of large quantities of lumber arriving at Pyote and being shunted onto rail sidings. Other unconfirmed reports told of construction crews being seen in town and of a major fencing project mysteriously underway around a huge tract of land just outside of the little city. Although every indication was that this activity had something to do with the as yet only rumored airfield, Ward County residents knew nothing for certain and continued to wait for confirmation of the rumors.[7]

On July 31, 1942, the *Monahans News* could at last firmly report that four sections of land had indeed been leased to the War Department and that this area was now being enclosed by miles of fence. A reporter had casually wandered onto the still unsecured property to observe "ten to fifteen box cars" full of lumber, some army trucks sitting idle, and a crew of men who "could be taken to be surveyors or engineers" at work. The paper also reported that the estimated construction cost of the airfield was to be $12 million "when and if" the work ever started.[8] As the total value of all Ward County had been appraised at $41 million just three years earlier, the long awaited official news that the air base was to become reality would obviously be warmly received.[9]

That welcome announcement was soon made, and on September 5, 1942, construction commenced. Unlike most other army airfields constructed in Texas in World War II, the facility at Pyote was unique in that there was nothing already built upon which to expand. No CAA survey teams had visited Pyote before the war simply because there was nothing there to survey. Prior to the war, no thought had apparently been given to the possibility of constructing an airfield near the all-but-deserted little town, and as there was no air facility of any kind already in place, there were obviously no existing runways to lengthen, no paved roads to widen, and no utility services to improve. At Pyote, there was nothing, except the thousands of acres of flat, sun-baked land that Commissioner Thomas had so convincingly extolled to the army's engineers.

There were, however, some other things on the University of Texas's land that Mr. Thomas had perhaps found good reason not to mention. There were thousands upon thousands of rattlesnakes. Construction workers were amazed at just how many of the writhing reptiles could be unearthed by the blades of the bulldozers. At the end of a work shift, the road grader operators would scrape what remained of the once dangerous snakes into huge piles, which would then be liberally soaked with a combination of diesel and gasoline and ignited. One old veteran recalled that the dead snakes seemed to continue to writhe and coil even as their funeral pyre consumed them.[10]

It did not require too many days of snake-killing and snake-burning to bring about the unofficial changing of Pyote Field's name to the Rattlesnake Bomber Base. Many soldiers who were eventually stationed at the facility incorrectly assumed that the name was only historical in nature. Much to their chagrin and often terror, the men soon discovered that rattlesnakes continued to dwell where hangars, storage buildings, and even barracks now stood. Soldiers who came to Pyote from the East and who were totally unfamiliar with such snakes were told by old timers to be careful when grasping airplane chock ropes, lest what appeared to be ropes have rattles on one end and deadly fangs on the other.[11]

Despite reptilian resistance, blinding dust and torrid heat, the construction of the base moved forward rapidly. In time, six huge hangars had been built, along with two runways over 8,400 feet long and 150 feet wide. Warehouses, railroad spurs, roadways, storage facilities, and living quarters soon appeared on the harsh landscape, and in less than a month after construction had started, army personnel began to arrive although the facility was less than half completed. Office workers were compelled to wear masks as protection from the dust that blew in open windows as the construction work continued. For a time, only one mess hall was available to feed everyone who was on the base. All officers, enlisted men, and construction workers dined in the cavernous and unfinished building that was devoid of heat or water.

The primary mission of Pyote Army Airfield was to train bombardment crews, and within just four months of its opening the base was the largest training facility of its kind in the United States. At its peak, the Pyote facility had a population of nearly 7,500.[12]

In town, the boom times had returned. Once again, new houses were hastily built and local citizens rented rooms in their homes to the civilian employees who could not be housed on the base. The population of the town grew to nearly 4,000, making it even larger than it had been in the oil boom days of the 1920s. Mr. H. C. Coursey, who was a boy when the airfield was at its peak, recalled that the sudden explosion in population on the base and in the town created what he termed "lots of steam." Coursey remembered that one of the locals' favorite pastimes was sitting "on the depot dock of a Saturday night and watching the fights that developed."[13]

The good citizens of Ward County took stern measures to

protect the town's young ladies from any unwelcomed contact with base personnel. In one of the more unique actions taken by a local government, the city council of nearby Monahans passed an ordinance that made it illegal for women to wear either shorts or swimsuits on the public streets. According to a story in the *San Antonio Express,* "Any cocky young officer with a thin mustache and a new convertible had it made," until the so-called cover-up rule went into effect.[14] Presumably, the town fathers reasoned that forbidding such provocative apparel would dampen the ardor of the boys from the base. No record exists to indicate if the ordinance had the desired effect or not, but another newspaper article reported that surprising support for the new law had been voiced by the community's "popular young set who work in local drugstores." One young lady proclaimed, "I'm glad they passed that ordinance, now we won't have to wait on some of those half-dressed fat squabs." Another member of the same set agreed, adding, "Sometimes I felt like popping some of them when they came around me all but undressed." The local church leaders perhaps predictably voiced their support of the so-called "Decency Order," as did a woman identified by the *Monahans News* only as a "paid-up subscriber." "Before the council passed the cover-up law," she wrote the editor, "I had found conditions in and around the city were becoming unbearable."[15]

On the base, there was likely precious little time to think about the charming if perhaps overdressed belles of Pyote. Although the sheer isolation of the facility often caused serious problems in morale, the rigorous training schedule kept both the flight and ground crews busy around the clock. Flying the hardworking Boeing B-17 bombers, the training crews achieved high standards of flying proficiency. In one month alone, the crews logged over 12,000 hours of flying time. Special service units provided excellent recreational activities for the crews that were not flying.

Contemporary photographs indicate that social functions on the airfield were occasionally high spirited affairs. The Officers' Club was the center of social activity for the commissioned flight crew members. Jackie Melton Fletcher, who was one of the first civilian employees on the base, recalled that the Officers' Club was a two-story building with a distinctly southern architectural styling. It boasted a hardwood dance floor and a balcony for those more interested in dining and drinking than in dancing. Parties at the club appear to have been relatively decorous events, with the ladies in attendance fashionably attired in long gowns and the officers themselves in their impeccable uniforms. A photo of the 1942 Christmas party at the enlisted men's club, however, strongly suggests that the festivities there were quite boisterous. The rather sodden-looking soldiers in the picture do not seem at all concerned with the correctness of their uniforms. Several of them clutch a beer bottle in each hand while many others appear to have emptied any number of bottles before the photograph was taken. Quite likely, even having a beer in each hand was not enough. It was Christmas, after all, and they were far from home, singing carols at Pyote, Texas.[16]

The holiday festivities over, the famed 19th Bombardment Group, which was to be the crew training school's cadre, arrived at Pyote on New Year's Day 1943. The group's B-17s settled onto their new base's long runways in fog and a cold drizzle. The weather was a dramatic change for the airmen who had flown directly to Pyote from the Pacific theater of war.

The 19th had been in the Philippines at the time of the Japanese invasion of those islands and had received a unit citation for its gallant action against the invaders from January 1 to March 1, 1942, and it had been the first unit to bomb Japanese targets in the war. Later, following additional combat in the Philippines, the Group had served with distinction against the enemy at Guadalcanal and in the air campaign against Rabaul, New Guinea.

Upon landing at Pyote, the 19th received its second presidential citation for its meritorious New Guinea action, presented by Maj. Gen. Robert Olds, an air force icon. During the same post-landing ceremony, General Olds awarded S.Sgt. Kenneth A. Gradle with a Silver Star, a Distinguished Flying Cross, and an Air Medal, making him the most decorated enlisted man in the entire United States Army at the time. As further evidence of the heroic effort put forth by the 19th in combat, its commanding officer, Lt. Col. Felix M. Hardison, had the distinction of being the most highly decorated officer in the army when the unit arrived in West Texas.[17]

The experienced bomber crews of the 19th served as instructors for less experienced pilots, navigators, and bombardiers who would soon be in combat themselves. Described by the local newspaper as being "renowned, battle-scarred [and] Jap-wise," the unit also proved to be very effective mentors.[18]

Despite the proficiency of the flight instructors, however, the twenty-four-hour-a-day training schedule took its toll. In a seven-day period in June 1943, nineteen aviators were killed when two B-17s crashed in separate incidents. In January 1945, flight instructor Lt. John Jamieson lost his life when he was hit by the turning propeller of a B-29. Jamieson, holder of the Distinguished Flying Cross and the Air Medal, was a veteran of twenty-five missions over Germany. He had just written his parents that he had requested a transfer back to the combat unit from which he had come since he found flying with the Eighth Air Force over Europe to be safer than being a flight instructor at Pyote. In spite of these unfortunate accidents, Pyote Airfield had a better safety record than most other installations, due largely to the fact that many of the crewmen training at the base were experienced fliers rather than cadets or raw primary trainees.[19]

On rare occasions, a seasoned pilot engaged in a display of irresponsibility that often cost him his commission. Second Lt. Rex A. Stage, for example, was cashiered from the army for simulating an attack on a bus full of civilians with his B-17 in March 1944. His misdeed was considered so flagrant that the court-martial findings that found him culpable were personally confirmed and endorsed by no less than President Franklin D. Roosevelt.

Lieutenant Stage explained to his jurors that bored with his daily training routine, he was "prompted by an irrepressible desire" to see what would happen if he flew at a very low altitude over a bus he had spotted on the highway below. He descended to within just feet of the rooftop of the bus, overtaking the vehicle from the rear. To slow his B-17 enough to not overshoot his quarry, Stage lowered his landing gear and extended the plane's flaps. To his consternation and reportedly to the abject terror of bus driver Tom Oliver and his twenty-eight passengers, the landing gear struck the top of the bus, inflicting only minor damage but completely unnerving its occupants. Although Lieutenant Stage absolved other crew members of any involvement in the decision to buzz the bus and maintaining that he did not intentionally strike it, he was nonetheless found guilty and dismissed from the service within ninety days of the incident.[20]

According to some old-time Pyote residents, other civilians were occasionally if inadvertently put in harm's way by the big airplanes that flew from Pyote Field. One memorable event seems to stand out in their collective memory as the prime example of the hazards of living close to a huge air base. A massed formation of hundreds of B-29s flying at tree-top level in a salute to a retiring army officer triggered a series of incidents on the ground. Mrs. J. W. Essary's goat was terrified by the noise and broke its neck attempting to escape from its pen. Frank Morales, who was shaving, cut his chin severely while his daughter Eva was scratched deeply by a cat she was holding. The whole Alaniz family panicked when the planes roared overhead and broke as a family unit for the front door of their house only to discover to their dismay that the narrow door was much too small to allow the nine children and two adults to pass through it simultaneously. Perhaps the most colorful if not downright suspicious tale concerning the strange events that occurred in Pyote on that memorable day is the one told by Mr. Caliche Wiley. According to him, his Siamese cat was so frightened by the roar of the low-flying aircraft that her tail became vertical and never again assumed its natural position. Mr. Wiley tried every cure he could think of to remedy the cat's unfortunate condition, including immersing it in gypsum water and massaging the affected area with hot oil, but the animal's tail remained erect for the rest of her long life. "It was really hard for that poor cat to sit down or even sleep," Mr. Wiley said, "but she always managed to eat okay."[21]

Fortunately for all concerned, both man and beast, such dramatic if noisy displays of America's air might were seldom staged at Pyote. Instead, the crews continued to train for combat until the end of the war. In December 1944, the war in Europe took an unexpected turn as German forces launched a desperate counter-offensive in the Ardennes. As a result, many enlisted men were transferred from their air duties at Pyote to infantry units requiring reinforcements following the costly Battle of the Bulge. The transfer created a serious morale problem on the airfield and was a source of considerable irritation to the base's senior officers.

In May 1945, following the capitulation of Nazi Germany, several hundred German prisoners of war arrived at Pyote, where only the WAC area and the flight line were declared off-limits to them. They were assigned to various labor details on the base, including a project to beautify the field's main entrance. The prisoners accomplished this task by creating a stone wall on either side of the main gate, complete with a large replica of an air force pilot's wings fashioned from solid rock.

In November 1945, the war in the Pacific was over and control of the Pyote facility was transferred from the Second Air Force to the Air Technical Command, headquartered in San Antonio. With this change of command, Pyote's colorful career as a final harbor for ghost airplanes was about to begin.

WHERE WAR BIRDS BECAME INGOTS

When all flight activity at the base was terminated, it became a storage depot for over 2,000 aircraft. Nearly every type of plane that had only recently helped win the war was flown to West Texas to be stored in the dry desert-like climate. There were B-29s and B-17s by the hundreds as well as B-25s, C-47s, P-51s, and many other models. Old-time Pyote residents can vividly remember seeing the long lines of stored aircraft stretching southward literally as far as the eye could see.

The most famous aircraft to arrive at Pyote for storage was the "Enola Gay," the plane that Col. Paul Tibbetts had flown on the atomic bomb raid over Hiroshima in August 1945. The airplane remained at Pyote until 1953 when it was flown to Washington for what would prove to be a forty-odd year period of preparation for eventual display at the Smithsonian's National Air and Space Museum.[22]

Also in storage at the base was "The Swoose," the only B-17 that had escaped destruction when the Philippine Islands had been overrun by the Japanese early in the war. "The Swoose," piloted by Maj. Frank P. Bostrom, had served as Gen. Douglas MacArthur's personal plane for a time. Later in the war, a naval officer from Texas, Lt. Cdr. Lyndon B. Johnson, had been on board "The Swoose" when it had made an emergency landing in Australia in 1943. The B-17 was also given to the Smithsonian after the war.[23]

Following the Korean War, all of the planes remaining at Pyote were dismantled and smelted down to become aluminum ingots. For a brief time, a radar monitoring site was maintained at the facility while the demolition of the massive surplus plane armada was in progress.

Finally, as the Ward County history book relates, "By 1966, time, weather, and vandals had taken their toll, and the Defense Department found it no longer economical to maintain such a remote facility."[24] County and city leaders had tried to save the base in order to minimize the economic decline that had already crippled the region immediately following the war. Despite their combined efforts, the land upon which the base had been built reverted to its original owner, the University of Texas, and the buildings were moved off the base or sold for scrap in 1976.

Little is left of the Rattlesnake Bomber Base today. The skeleton of the sole remaining hangar can be glimpsed from the highway, and the main gate wall built by the German prisoners remains intact, its wings of stone still in place. Beyond the wall itself is an old turnstile through which once passed the thousands of airmen on their way into Pyote or returning to base, perhaps after an evening of revelry.

There is little occasion for revelry in Pyote today. The tiny community is at the very nadir of its unfortunate but seemingly persistent cycle of boom and bust. Only three hundred people reside in the town now and just a handful of small businesses have survived the economic collapse that began with the closing of the airfield. On the outskirts of town, however, in a building moved from the base in 1966, a museum preserves the memories of Pyote Army Airfield and the men who served there. A yellowing collection of half-century-old photographs present an almost ghostly image of what life was like on the now vanished military facility.

All of Pyote's legacies are not dead, however. Along the stretch of Interstate 20 that passes close to what was once the north end of one of the airfield's main runways, state horticulturists not long ago were surprised to find a rare weed rapidly spreading across the barren desert soil. The dark green plant with small white blossoms was eventually identified as a rare variety of African Rue, a plant known to grow naturally only on that far-off continent. The perplexed experts finally surmised that the seeds of the plant had somehow found their way onto the landing gear of B-29s taking off from African bases bound for Texas during the war.

As the giant planes lowered their gear to land into the prevailing southerly winds at Pyote, the seeds blew off and drifted to the earth under the approach path of the Superfortresses. After a long period of dormancy, the seeds finally germinated, sprouted, and began to spread vigorously. To their dismay, local ranchers soon discovered that the weed was poisonous to cattle, but concerted efforts to eradicate the invading plant have been in vain. Unlike the mighty aircraft that carried it to Texas so long ago, the African Rue has refused to die. Its mere presence, no matter how unwanted, is one of the very few living reminders of the once worldwide reach of the Rattlesnake Bomber Base at Pyote, Texas.[25]

Col. John R. Morgan, shown at the extreme left, was Harlingen Aerial Gunnery School's first commander. He is shown being greeted by his entire officer corps upon making the first landing at the field.
— Courtesy, *Valley Morning Star*, Harlingen, Texas

A vintage photograph of the main gate at Harlingen early in the war shows its often misunderstood and mirth-provoking acronym sign in place on the gatehouse roof.
— Courtesy, *Valley Morning Star*, Harlingen, Texas

Although little remains of the airfield's original buildings today, Harlingen was clearly an impressive facility fifty years ago.
— U.S. Air Force Photo

A CAMERA TRIP THROUGH "HAGS"
HARLINGEN ARMY GUNNERY SCHOOL

An apparently staged studio shot depicts a very determined aerial gunner at work. This same photograph was also used on the covers of guidebooks distributed by other airfields during the war.
— Courtesy, Texas Air Museum. Rio Hondo, Texas

The Waller Trainer at Harlingen's Gunnery School simulated attacking enemy aircraft by means of realistic movie projections.
— U.S. Air Force Photo. Used by permission of the
University of Texas Institute of Texan Cultures at San Antonio

Despite countless local rumors to the contrary, Clark Gable was never stationed at Harlingen, although he was an actual Air Force gunner. Here, a self-styled stand-in and his extremely bored puppy easily dispel the rumor.
— Courtesy, Texas Air Museum. Rio Hondo, Texas

*Lt. Col. John L. Kottal (center) as an enlisted man at Harlingen in 1942
developed an ingenious technique for distributing the base's grapefruit crop
to his fellow sentries. Colonel Kottal is shown here at his retirement
ceremony in 1961.*

— *Harlingen Press.* Harlingen, Texas

Aircraft from the Harlingen Aerial Gunnery School fly in formation over the field's main gate in 1942 for the benefit of Paramount's movie cameras on location to film "Aerial Gunner."

— Courtesy, Harlingen Public Library

Actors Chester Morris, Jimmy Lydon, and Richard Arlen pose at Harlingen Field's Main Gate during the filming of the motion picture "Aerial Gunner."

This view of Pyote, Texas, probably never decorated a post card.
— Courtesy, Ward County Historical Association Archives, Monahans, Texas

Few traffic lights were required in downtown Pyote.
— Courtesy, Ward County Historical Association Archives, Monahans, Texas

Even though the base was yet to be officially announced, lumber began arriving at Pyote.
— Courtesy, Ward County Historical Association Archives, Monahans, Texas

Despite such primitive equipment, Pyote Airfield was built in record time.
— Courtesy, Ward County Historical Association Archives, Monahans, Texas

Rattlesnake Bomber Base was obviously appropriately named.
— Courtesy, Ward County Historical Association Archives, Monahans, Texas

The Main Gate to the Rattlesnake Bomber Base at Pyote bid welcome to thousands of soldiers.
— Courtesy, Ward County Historical Association Archives, Monahans, Texas

Though nothing remains of it today, Pyote Field was mammoth long ago.
— Courtesy, Ward County Historical Association Archive, Monahans, Texas

Still under construction, the field was less than photogenic.
— Courtesy, Ward County Historical Association Archives, Monahans, Texas

*Rattlesnake Bomber Base's flight operations set training records
that were never equaled.*
— Courtesy, Ward County Historical Association Archives, Monahans, Texas

The 19th Bomb Group's B-17s fly in really low altitude formation as more decorations are awarded.
— Courtesy, Ward County Historical Association Archives, Monahans, Texas

AMERICA'S MOST BEMEDALED FIGHTING AIRMEN

The much decorated 19th Bomb Group donned Class A uniforms to receive even more medals in 1943.
— Courtesy, Ward County Historical Association Archives, Monahans, Texas

*Walt Disney Studios designed the official insignia for Pyote Field Base
Training Unit. While the saguaro cactus depicted does not grow anywhere
near Pyote, the rattlesnake most certainly does . . . and often to great lengths.*
— Courtesy, Ward County Historical Association Archives, Monahans, Texas

Awash in Schlitz beer, G.I. Joes celebrate Christmas at Pyote, 1942.
— Courtesy, Ward County Historical Association Archives, Monahans, Texas

The NCOs celebrated the same holiday with a bit more restraint than the boys shown above.
— Courtesy, Ward County Historical Association Archives, Monahans, Texas

The officers and their wives make the most of Christmas at Pyote, in 1942.
— Courtesy, Ward County Historical Association Archives, Monahans, Texas

*Once Gen. Douglas MacArthur's personal plane, "The Swoose"
came to Pyote after the war.*
— Courtesy, Ward County Historical Association Archives, Monahans, Texas

Although shown in "mothballs," "The Swoose" escaped postwar destruction and went to the Smithsonian.
— Courtesy, Ward County Historical Association Archives, Monahans, Texas

Pyote's most famous guest, "The Enola Gay" eventually went on display at the National Air and Space Museum.
— Courtesy, Ward County Historical Association Archives, Monahans, Texas

No longer needed, many B-29s await destruction in
Pyote's smelters after the war.
— Courtesy, Ward County Historical Association Archives, Monahans, Texas

As the planes were being destroyed, the hangars fell into great disrepair.
— Courtesy, Ward County Historical Association Archives, Monahans, Texas

By the late 1970s, the destruction of the base was all but total.
— Courtesy, Ward County Historical Association Archives, Monahans, Texas

The base gone, this still standing turnstile at the gate never turns.
— Courtesy, Ward County Historical Association Archives, Monahans, Texas

Texas Historical Commission Marker
In the great vastness of West Texas, at what was once the main gate to the sprawling old air base, the Ward County Historical Association-sponsored Texas historical marker tells the story of what happened here fifty years ago.
— Author's Photograph

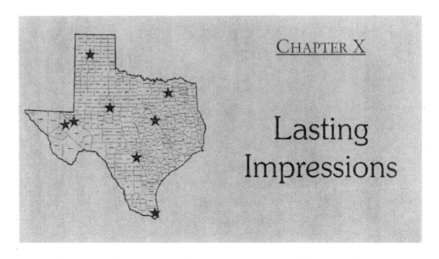

Chapter X

Lasting Impressions

When World War II at last came to an end late in the summer of 1945, nearly all Texans were eager to forget the horrors of war and move forward into what it was hoped would be a peaceful second half of the twentieth century. What had only recently been a massive and very visible military presence in the state diminished rapidly, and soon little physical evidence of the great war was readily apparent. In the decade that followed, however, a few fading reminders of what had been the largest military undertaking in the state's history could still be discerned.

Many of the narrow barrier islands along the Gulf of Mexico were pockmarked by craters gouged in the sand by practice bombs dropped from training aircraft. Once bustling army airfields stood deserted and unfenced, virtually inviting vandals to accelerate the vast destruction already created by time and weather. Giant hangars that had not long before housed sleek winged weapons of war were without either roofs or doors and now home to only pigeons, spiders, and rats. Alongside abandoned runways, a weathered tetrahedron might be seen as it turned eerily on its axis as if to indicate the wind's direction to some ghostly air force plane that would never land.

The aviation trainees who came to Texas during the Korean War in the early 1950s also found some evidence of the much larger conflict that had ended a few years earlier. A handful of Mitchell B-25 bombers that had survived combat missions over Germany and Japan now served as training planes carrying a new generation of student bombardiers and navigators through the skies of Texas. Many of those same students had been issued quaint World War II vintage leather flying helmets that still bore the proud wing and star insignia of the old Army Air Force on their basset-hound ear flaps. Hot and uncomfortable, the helmets were customarily worn only while drinking beer in an air-conditioned room at the Bachelor Officers' Quarters.

Although time would soon erase most of the remaining visible reminders of the war, the effect of it on the Texans themselves would prove to be far more enduring. World War II had opened wide the invisible but nonetheless very real gates that for decades had held back the forces of change. Throughout the Lone Star State, the old closed social order was fading rapidly, being replaced by a far more modern, open-minded, and freer society born of war. To be sure, there were those who refused to recognize that the war-caused invasion of nearly a million servicemen and women had brought twentieth century thinking to many of the previously more isolated parts of Texas. There were a few hard-bitten old curmudgeons who likely would not have believed anything had changed even if Adolf Hitler himself had triumphantly ridden in the grand entry parade at the local rodeo. Most postwar Texans, however, accepted the fact that their traditional way of life had been reshaped, and for the most part favorably so, by the effects of the war. They accepted the changes philosophically but not always without some reservations.

It can of course be conclusively argued that the state of Texas eventually would have changed anyway, war or no war. In time, it would have been propelled into the twentieth century by the emergence of such undeniable forces as immigration, better education, mass communication, and vastly improved transportation. However, there can be no question that World War II significantly accelerated what was likely an inevitable change in the manner in which many Texans thought and in the way they had lived for generations. In short, the war literally flung open a door that under less dramatic conditions might have swung open only slowly and with great caution.

There were two fundamental factors of the change created by the war. One was simply the massive influx into the state of nearly one million strangers with varying perspectives on many wide-ranging social issues including racial and gender equality, respect for law and order, archaic rules governing the sale of alcoholic beverages, and morality in general. To many of the newcomers, anything that felt like real fun in rural Texas was either considered immoral by the church folks or illegal by the sheriffs. The often stringent ground rules for social behavior were constantly being probed, tested, and often bent by the high-spirited and free-thinking individuals who had come to Texas only because some much higher authority had ordered them to do so. As a group, therefore, they were not particularly much inclined to warmly embrace locally conceived frontier codes of conduct which were often perceived as being bucolic if not downright primitive in nature. The newcomers' challenges to the established social order often served as an enlightenment and eventually brought about a modernizing and lasting change in many long standing traditions.

The second fundamental element of change brought about by the war was economic. It is abundantly clear that the sudden infusion of new federal capital liberally lubricated the wheels of progress in Texas during the war years. Out of the economic stagnation of the Great Depression grew a prosperity fueled chiefly by the construction of multimillion-dollar military installations across the state. Army payrolls on the new or enlarged facilities added a regularity to the generation of income that had long been absent from the Texas economy. Civilian support of the military installations and their personnel gave reliable and good paying employment to many workers in the smaller towns, while major wartime industrial jobs in the larger cities provided a degree of compensation virtually unparalleled in the history of the state.

Not everyone grew wealthy because of the war by any stretch of the imagination, but the diminution of poverty and the concomitant rise in the overall standard of living contributed to the acceptance, or at least tolerance, of the huge military force that had come to Texas. The army's personnel might have broken some laws and impudently challenged the old social routines, but more important, the army itself had also brought cash to communities that had previously been just barely subsisting on barter, good will, and rapidly diminishing lines of credit from banks soon likely to fail.

The military personnel who had temporarily come to Texas from other states during the war were by no means the only ones to cause things to change. The many homecoming Texas veterans themselves were also instrumental in redefining the state following the war. These former soldiers and sailors had seen and done things they would have very likely neither seen nor done had there not been a war. They probably would have stayed close to their homes forever, but instead they had viewed the world and its people on a grand scale, and for many of them their wartime experience would be the highlight of their lives. In short, they were not the same as they had once been, and it simply was not possible for them to ever fully accept their hometowns and the people in them as they had been before the war came. What the massive influx of out-of-state servicemen had first put in motion in 1941 was expanded by the returning Texan veterans in 1945. As a direct result of these collective new attitudes and perspectives, Texas moved away from the restrictive society that had been firmly in place for over a century and moved toward an enlightened future.

There were others who helped change the face of the Lone Star State. Many service personnel from other states had found much to like in Texas while they were stationed in it, even though some who had come from larger and more cosmopolitan cities often found the rural areas of the state to be almost hopelessly rustic in both thought and deed. After V-J Day, a surprisingly large number of these out-of-state veterans began moving with their families to Texas. San Antonio and Harlingen gained the larger share of those who had decided to become permanent Texans. Bexar and Cameron counties, representing San Antonio and Harlingen respectively, both experienced a population increase in excess of 50 percent from 1940 to 1950. Overall, the state posted an increase of 20 percent for the same period, while the western part had a less robust growth than the overall average.

However, it is in West Texas where the most poignant lasting impressions of the World War II air force can still be found. Bases that once thrived in Pecos, Pyote, and Amarillo, for example, have all but dissolved. A few rotting buildings and the peeling remnants of runways are all that physically remain of what was once a massive and concentrated human endeavor. Although the men and their machines of war are long gone, there is something of an aura about the old bases that is not too unlike that which hovers over other such haunted places as Gettysburg and Normandy Beach. It is almost palpable, a feeling that perhaps all of that intense human and mechanical energy and activity of over fifty years ago is just too immense to ever dissolve as the hangars and the runways have.

On all but three of the old airfields covered in this book, there is only that wispy and elusive aura to indicate that a mighty base existed there and that thousands once served on it. At least Pyote, Majors, and Avenger Fields each have historical markers to provide information about the base and to serve as something of a memorial to the countless servicemen and women who were stationed there. Randolph Air Force Base, the sole active survivor of the bases visited in this text, needs no state-supplied metal marker to tell of its history and importance. Randolph is itself a living monument to the air force and its contribution to Texas.

The other airfields, however, are unmarked, save for rusting fences and weathered water towers. The Texas Historical Commission signs are not difficult to obtain if the supporting documents are found to be worthy. What could possibly be more deserving of permanent recognition than a place where long ago, many lived, some died, and all came together to help win a war!

According to a Knight-Ridder news report, veterans of that war were dying at the rate of one thousand per day at the end of the twentieth century. It would seem highly fitting if every once vital military installation that had existed during World War II could be suitably honored with an historical marker before all of those who had been posted there become history themselves. For a small amount of effort and money, both history and the men and women who came to Texas during World War II would be well served.

Although much of the physical evidence of the World War II

experience in Texas has been destroyed, the natural setting of it all remains eternally the same. It is still possible to find uncrowded places from which to watch the fiery setting sun ignite the heavens just as Lucy Kuykendall at Pecos and Charlotte Mitchell at Avenger Field did so many years ago. Away from city lights, the brilliant red, orange, and purple colorations of those sunsets seem to be reluctant to fade to a darkness studded with countless bright stars. Standing near an abandoned runway on a deserted wartime airfield, it is easy to imagine how it might have been during World War II when countless stars etched on the wingtips of army airplanes shared those skies.

Both in the stark reality of war and in memories now softly burnished by the gentle passage of time, all the stars over Texas were big and bright.

Appendices

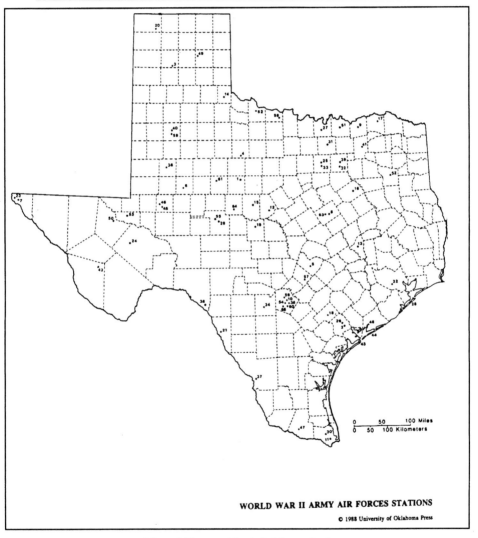

Map of Texas with airfields marked.
Copyright © 1988. Historical Atlas of Texas.
The University of Oklahoma Press. Used by permission.

211

World War II Army Air Forces Stations

The wide expanse of relatively level terrain, coupled with a large number of clear weather days, enabled Texas to become a major location for the establishment of Army Air Forces stations. The federal government started new flying fields and contracted for the use of existing municipal facilities to meet the need for trained pilots, navigators, bombardiers, and maintenance personnel during World War II. These installations had an influence on local services and life-styles and brought about changes to communities much more quickly than would have occurred under traditional conditions.

When the conflict ended, the federal government made some of the fields a permanent part of the national defense system and transferred other properties to local governments. These acquisitions of improved air power facilities by municipalities and counties led to a marked increase in aviation for agriculture, business, commerical traffic, industry, and personal flying pleasure.

The following list provides the names and locations of Army Air Force stations in Texas during World War II:

Army Air Forces Station	Location
1. Abilene Army Air Field	Abilene
2. Aloe Army Air Field	Victoria
3. Amarillo Army Air Field	Amarillo
4. Arledge Field	Stamford
5. Bergstrom Field	Austin
6. Big Spring Army Air Field	Big Spring
7. Biggs Field	El Paso
8. Blackland Army Air Field	Waco
9. Bonham Municipal Airport	Bonham
10. Brooks Field	San Antonio
11. Brownsville Municipal Airport	Brownsville
12. Brownwood Army Air Field	Brownsville
13. Bryan Army Air Field	Bryan
14. Childress Army Air Field	Childress
15. Coleman Flying School	Coleman
16. Corsicana Field	Corsicana
17. Cox Field	Paris
18. Cuero Municipal Airport	Cuero
19. Curtis Field	Brady
20. Dalhart Army Air Field	San Antonio
21. Eagle Pass Army Air Field	Eagle Pass
22. Ellington Field	Houston
23. El Paso Municipal Airport	El Paso
24. Fort Stockton Field	Fort Stockton

25.	Fort Worth Army Air Field	Fort Worth
26.	Foster Field	Victoria
27.	Gainesville Army Air Field	Gainesville
28.	Galveston Army Air Field	Galveston
29.	Goodfellow Field	San Angelo
30.	Harlingen Army Air Field	Harlingen
31.	Hartlee Field	Denton
32.	Hensley Field	Dallas
33.	Hicks Field	Fort Worth
34.	Hondo Army Air Field	Hondo
35.	Kelly Field	San Antonio
36.	Lamesa Municipal Airport	Lamesa
37.	Laredo Army Air Field	Laredo
38.	Laughlin Field	Del Rio
39.	Love Field	Dallas
40.	Lubbock Army Air Field	Lubbock
41.	Majors Field	Greenville
42.	Marfa Army Air Field	Marfa
43.	Matagorda Island Bombing and Gunnery Range	Victoria
44.	Matagorda Peninsula Bombing Range	Childress
45.	Midland Army Air Field	Midland
46.	Midland Municipal Airport	Midland
47.	Moore Field	Mission
48.	Palacios Army Air Field	Palacios
49.	Pampa Army Air Field	Pampa
50.	Pecos Army Air Field	Pecos
51.	Perrin Field	Sherman
52.	Pounds Field	Tyler
53.	Pyote Army Air Field	Pyote
54.	Randolph Field	San Antonio
55.	San Angelo Army Air Field	San Angelo
56.	San Antonio Municipal Airport	San Antonio
57.	San Marcos Army Air Field	San Marcos
58.	Sheppard Field	Wichita Falls
59.	South Plains Army Air Field	Lubbock
60.	Stinson Field	San Antonio
61.	Sweetwater Municipal Airport	Sweetwater
62.	Victory Field	Vernon
63.	Waco Army Air Field	Waco
64.	Bruce Field	Ballinger
65.	San Antonio Aviation Cadet Center (Lackland Army Air Field, 1946)	San Antonio

— Courtesy, *Historical Atlas of Texas*
Copyright © 1988
The University of Oklahoma Press. Used by Permission.

Amarillo Army Airfield

U.S. Army Air Force Information Sheets
April 1945 (Formerly Restricted)

SIZE: 677 acres (total area).

LANDING AREA: Runways: N/S 4,895' x 150', NE/SW 5,022' x 150', NW/SE 5,014' x 150', asphalt concrete.

APPROACH HAZARDS: None within 40/1 glide angle, except N 20/1.

LIGHTING: Beacon (rotating and code); obst.; B-2 runway (portable); flood (stationary boundary; contact; range; approach; and mobile).

HANGARS: (4) 326' x 163', door 120' x 28'; (1) 163' x 163' door 120' x 28' steel.

SHOPS: Major engine repair, major aircraft repair.

GASOLINE: At Airport - 87, 91, and 100 octane; 10 servicing trucks.
In Vicinity - None reported.

OIL: At Airport - Available.
In Vicinity - 50.0 mi.

RADIO FACILITIES:
RANGE -251 kcs.; ident. "AQ"; mag. bearing and distance, station to field, 77°, 2.0 mi.
TOWER 278 kcs. and 126.18 mcs. (Cont.).
GND/AIR - WZP (ACCS).
INSTRUMENT APPROACH AND LETDOWN PROCE-DURE - Min. safe initial approach alt. N and S min. en route alt. E 5,000' (int. SE leg DPW); W 5,500' (TC Range Station). Final approach, W. leg. Procedure turn alt., S side 5.0-10.0-15.0 mi. 5,000'; 20.0-25.0 mi. 5,500'. Alt. over range, final approach, 4,300'. Min. safe letdown alt. over field, estab-lished by using agency. Missed approach, over field, established by using agency, proceed out E leg climbing to 5,000'.

WEATHER: (Records from Station at Amarillo):
PREVAILING WIND-S, except Nov., Dec., Jan., Feb., Mar., SW.
PRECIPITATION - Av. mo., 0.49" (Jan.) to 3.20" (Aug.); av. yr., 21.59".
TEMPERATURE - Av. min. and max., 44° to 69°; extremes, -16° to 106°.
FOG - Not prevalent.

FACILITIES (At Airport) - First order weather station; CAA weather teletype, 24-hr. operation.

TRANSPORTATION:
AIRLINES - Braniff Airways; Transcontinental & Western Air, Inc.
RAILROADS - Chicago, Rock Island & Pacific; Fort Worth & Denver City; Panhandle & Santa Fe; at Amarillo. Sidings - 3,000' in lgth., adjacent N.
ROADS - U.S. Nos. 60, adjacent N; U.S. No. 66, adjacent S; paved.
FACILITIES - Bus and taxi service.

COMMUNICATIONS: Telephone; telegraph; teletype.

PERSONNEL ACCOMMODA-TIONS (Transient):
At Airport - 30 officers; 50 enlisted men.
In Vicinity - Amarillo

Avenger Field

U.S. Army Air Force Information Sheets
April 1945 (Formerly Restricted)

SIZE: 943 acres (total area).

LANDING AREA: Runways: N/S 6,200' x 150', NE/SW 6,200' x 150', NW/SE 6,200' x 150', asphalt (under const.). All-way area: N/S 5,500' x E/W 400' to 2,000', caliche.

APPROACH HAZARDS: None within 40/1 glide angle.

LIGHTING: Beacon (rotating; obst.; boundary; contact; range.

HANGARS: (2) 200' x 160', door 100' x 16' wood; (2) 200' x 140' door 100' x 16'; (1) 105' x 90', door 90' x 16'; (1) 100' x 90', door 90' x 18' steel.

SHOPS: Minor engine repair, minor aircraft repair.

GASOLINE:
At Airport - 73, 91, and 100 octane; 4 servicing trucks.
In Vicinity - None reported.

OIL:
At Airport - SAE 60.
In Vicinity - None reported.

RADIO FACILITIES:
RANGE - None.
TOWER 219 kcs. and 125.18 mcs. (0600-2400).
GND/AIR - None.
INSTRUMENT APPROACH AND LETDOWN PROCEDURE - None.

WEATHER:
PREVAILING WIND - No data.
PRECIPITATION - No data.
TEMPERATURE - No data.
FOG - No data.
FACILITIES (At Airport) - First order weather station; Army weather teletype, 24-hr. operation.

TRANSPORTATION:
AIRLINES - None reported.
RAILROADS - Gulf, Colorado & Santa Fe; Panhandle & Santa Fe; Texas & Pacific; at Sweetwater.
Sidings - Capacity, 3 cars, adjacent.
ROADS - U.S. Nos. 80 and 84, adjacent S. paved.
FACILITIES - Bus and taxi service.

COMMUNICATIONS: Telephone; telegraph; teletype.

PERSONNEL ACCOMMODA- TIONS (Transient):
At Airport - None.
In Vicinity - At Sweetwater

Harlingen Army Airfield

U.S. Army Air Force Information Sheets
April 1945 (Formerly Restricted)

SIZE: 1,494 acres (total area).

LANDING AREA: Runways: (2) N/S 6,000' x 150', NE/SW 5,200' x 150', E/W 5,200' x 150', NW/SE 5,200' x 150' concrete.

APPROACH HAZARDS: None within 40/1 glide angle.

LIGHTING: Beacon (rotation); obst.; contact; B-2 runway (portable); flood (stationary).

HANGARS: (2) 184' x 120', door 183' x 20' steel; (1) 154' x 85', door 120' x 24' tile and concrete.

SHOPS: Major engine repair; major aircraft repair.

GASOLINE:
At Airport - 91 and 100 octane.
In Vicinity - 100 octane, 25.0 mi. (air line).

OIL:
At Airport - Available.
In Vicinity - 25.0 mi. (air line).

RADIO FACILITIES:
RANGE -None.
TOWER - 368 kics. and 126.18 mcs. (Cont.).
GND/AIR - None.
INSTRUMENT APPROACH AND LETDOWN PROCEDURE - None.

WEATHER (Records from Station at Harlingen):

PREVAILING WIND-SE.

PRECIPITATION - Av. mo., 1.03" (Apr.) to 5.34" (Sept.); av. yr., 26.17".

TEMPERATURE - Av. min. and max., 62.4° to 84.4°; extremes, 22° to 108°.

FOG - Early morning.

FACILITIES (At Airport)-
First-order weather station; Army weather teletype, 24-hr. operation.

TRANSPORTATION:
AIRLINES - None reported.
RAILROADS - Missouri Pacific; Southern Pacific; at Harlingen.
Sidings - On field.
ROADS - State No. 96, 3.6 mi. WSW, paved; county road, adjacent S, improved.
FACILITIES - Bus and taxi service.

COMMUNICATIONS: Telephone telegraph; teletype.

PERSONNEL ACCOMMODATIONS (Transient):
At Airport - 30 Officers; 200 enlisted men.
In Vicinity - At Harlingen.

Harlingen Army Airfield Auxiliary
(Laguna Madre Gunnery Range)

U.S. Army Air Force Information Sheets
April 1945 (Formerly Restricted)

SIZE: 10,168 acres (total area).
LANDING AREA: Runways: N/S
4,000' x 150', E/W 4,000' x 150',
NW/SE 4,750' x 150', concrete.
APPROACH HAZARDS: None
within 40/1 glide angle.
LIGHTING: Obst.
HANGARS: None.
SHOPS: None.
GASOLINE:
At Airport - 91 octane; 3
servicing trucks.
In Vicinity - At Harlingen Army
Air Field.
OIL:
At Airport - Available.
In Vicinity - At Harlingen Army
Air Field.
RADIO FACILITIES:
RANGE -None.
TOWER - None.
GND/AIR - None.
INSTRUMENT APPROACH
AND LETDOWN
PROCEDURE - None.

WEATHER:
PREVAILING WIND-No data.
PRECIPITATION - Av. mo.,
0.37" (Aug.) to 3.25" (Oct.);
av. yr., 26.17".
TEMPERATURE - No data.
FOG - Not prevalent.
FACILITIES (At Airport)-
None.
TRANSPORTATION:
AIRLINES - None reported.
RAILROADS - Missouri
Pacific; Southern Pacific; at
Harlingen.
Sidings - 1.5 mi. from field.
ROADS - State No. 100, 5.0 mi.
S, paved; county road, ad-
jacent W, improved.
FACILITIES - Bus service.
COMMUNICATIONS: Telephone.
PERSONNEL ACCOMMODA-
TIONS (Transient):
At Airport - None.
In Vicinity - At Harlingen.

Majors Field
Greenville

SIZE: 1,504 acres.

RUNWAYS: N/S 5,500' x 150', N/S 5,000' x 150', E/W 5,500' x 150', NW/SE 5,500' x 150' concrete.

APPROACH HAZARDS: None within 40/1 glide angle.

LIGHTING: Beacon (rotating); obst.; contact; runway (mobile).

HANGARS: (2) 140' x 110', door 100' x 16', metal

SHOPS: Major repairs.

GASOLINE:

At Airport - 87, 91, and 100 octane; tank capacity, 220,000 gal.; 16 servicing trucks, total capacity, 32,000 gal..

In Vicinity - None reported.

OIL:

At Airport - SAE 10 to 60, 32,000 qt., in tanks.

In Vicinity - None reported.

RADIO FACILITIES:

RANGE -None.

TOWER - 272 kcs.; continuous.

INSTRUMENT APPROACH AND LETDOWN PROCEDURE - None.

WEATHER:

PREVAILING WIND-S, except Nov., Dec., Jan., Feb., N; Oct., E.

PRECIPITATION - Av. mo., 2.24" (Feb.) to 4.70" (May); av. yr., 37.63".

TEMPERATURE - Av. min. and max., 53.4° to 76.6°; extremes, -4° to 115°.

FOG - Not prevalent.

FACILITIES Class A weather station.

TRANSPORTATION:

AIRLINES - None reported.

RAILROADS - Louisiana & Arkansas; Missouri-Kansas-Texas; St. Louis Southwestern; Southern Pacific; at Greenville. Sidings - On field.

ROADS - U.S. No. 69, 1.5 mi. NE; county road, adjacent NW; paved.

FACILITIES - Bus and taxi service.

COMMUNICATIONS: Telephone; telegraph; teletype; AACS station, call WXSY.

PERSONNEL ACCOMMODA-TIONS:

At Airport - 15 Officers; 75 enlisted men.

In Vicinity - At Greenville.

Pecos Army Air Field
Pecos

SIZE: 1,933 acres.

RUNWAYS: N/S 6,200' x 150', E/W 7,200' x 150', NNW/SSE 6,200' x 150', asphalt.

APPROACH HAZARDS: None within 40/1 glide angle.

LIGHTING: Beacon (rotating); obst.; landing strip; range; runway (mobile); flood.

HANGARS: (1) 200' x 162', door wdth. 120'; (2) 160' x 130', door 54' x 14'; (1) 122' x 80', door wdth. 120'.

SHOPS: Minor repairs.

GASOLINE:
At Airport - 87 to 91 octane, 160,000 gal.; tank capacity, 198,000 gal.; 7 servicing trucks.
In Vicinity - At Pecos.

OIL:
At Airport - 24,000 qt., in underground storage.
In Vicinity - At Pecos.

RADIO FACILITIES:
RANGE -None.
TOWER - None.
INSTRUMENT APPROACH AND LETDOWN PROCEDURE - None.

WEATHER:
PREVAILING WIND-SE, except Dec., Jan., Feb., Mar., Apr., W; Sept., S.
PRECIPITATION - Av. mo., 0.18" (Jan.) to 1.86" (Sept.); av. yr., 10.64".
TEMPERATURE - Av. min. and max., 48.7° to 80.2°; extremes, -4° to 114°.
FOG - Dec., Jan., Feb.
FACILITIES Class B weather station.

TRANSPORTATION:
AIRLINES - None reported.
RAILROADS - Panhandle & Santa Fe; Pecos Valley Southern; Texas & Pacific; at Pecos. Sidings - On field.
ROADS - U.S. No. 80, 2.0 mi. N; U.S. No. 285, 1.75 mi. E; State No. 17, adjacent W; paved.
FACILITIES - Bus service.

COMMUNICATIONS: Telephone; telegraph; teletype.

PERSONNEL ACCOMMODATIONS:
At Airport - 10 Officers; 300 enlisted men.
In Vicinity - At Pecos.

Pyote Army Airfield

U.S. Army Air Force Information Sheets
April 1945 (Formerly Restricted)

SIZE: 2,745 acres (total area).

LANDING AREA: Runways: N/S 8,400' x 150', E/W 8,522' x 150', NW/SE 8,400' x 150', asphalt.

APPROACH HAZARDS: None within 40/1 glide angle.

LIGHTING: Beacon (rotating); obst.; contact; approach; B-2 runway (portable); flood (stationary).

HANGARS: (1) 253' x 210', door 158'6" x 36'; (4) 220' x 117', door 160' x 36'9" wood and concrete.

SHOPS: Major engine repair, major aircraft repair.

GASOLINE:
At Airport - 91, and 100 octane; 13 servicing trucks.
In Vicinity - None reported.

OIL:
At Airport - Available.
In Vicinity - None reported.

RADIO FACILITIES:
RANGE - 287 kcs.; ident. "DPY"; mag. bearing and distance, station to field, 120°, 3.9 mi.
TOWER 272 kcs. and 126.18 mcs. (Cont.).
GND/AIR - None.
INSTRUMENT APPROACH AND LETDOWN PROCE DURE - Min. safe initial ap proach alt., NE 6,000' (int. NE leg WP): SE 6,000' (int. SE leg WP); SW min. en route

alt.; NW 6,000' (int. W leg WP). Final approach, NW leg. Procedure turn alt., S side 4,100'. Alt. over range, final approach, 3,400'. Min. safe letdown alt. over field, established by using agency. Missed approach, pro ceed out SE leg climbing to 6,000'.

WEATHER:
PREVAILING WIND - No data.
PRECIPITATION - No data.
TEMPERATURE - No data.
FOG - Nov., Dec., Jan.
FACILITIES (At Airport) - Class A weather station; Army weather teletype, 24-hr. operation.

TRANSPORTATION:
AIRLINES - None reported.
RAILROADS - Texas & Pacific; at Pyote. Sidings - 6,341' in lgth., on field.
ROADS - U.S. No. 80, 0.5 mi. N; State No. 115, 0.8 mi. NE; paved.
FACILITIES - Bus service.

COMMUNICATIONS: Telephone; telegraph; teletype.

PERSONNEL ACCOMMODA- TIONS (Transient):
At Airport - 50 officers; 50 enlisted men.
In Vicinity - At Pyote.

Randolph Army Airfield

U.S. Army Air Force Information Sheets
April 1945 (Formerly Restricted)

SIZE: 2,318 acres (total area).

LANDING AREA: Runways: (2) NW/SE 5,500' x 150', concrete.

APPROACH HAZARDS: None within 40/1 glide angle except NW 35/1.

LIGHTING: Beacon (undulating); obst.; boundary contact; B-2 runway (portable); flood (stationary and mobile).

HANGARS: (15) 220' x 110', door 110' x 21'10".

SHOPS: Major engine repair, major aircraft repair.

GASOLINE:
At Airport - 73, 87, 91, and 100 octane; 19 servicing trucks.
In Vicinity - SAE 60, 40.0 mi.

OIL:
At Airport - SAE 60.
In Vicinity - SAE 60, 40.0 mi.

RADIO FACILITIES:
RANGE - 359 kcs.; ident. "DRQQ"; mag. bearing and distance, station to field, 322°, 2.04 mi.
TOWER 272 kcs. and 126.18 mcs. (Cont.).
GND/AIR - None.
INSTRUMENT APPROACH AND LETDOWN PROCEDURE - Min. safe initial approach alt., NE 2,000' (int. S leg DMS): SE min. en route alt.; SW 2,100' (int. S leg JR); NW 2,500' (int. N leg JR). Final approach, SE leg. Procedure turn alt., E side 2,000'. Alt. over range, final approach, 1,500'. Min. safe letdown alt. over field, established by using agency. Missed approach, proceed out NW leg climbing to 2,5000'.

WEATHER: (Records from Station at San Antonio):
PREVAILING WIND - SE, except Nov., Dec., Jan., N; Feb., NE.
PRECIPITATION - Av. mo., 1.34" (Jan.) to 3.24" (Sept.); av. yr., 27.39".
TEMPERATURE - Av. min. and max., 58.8° to 79.3°; extremes, 4° to 107°.
FOG - Dec., Feb., Mar., Apr.
FACILITIES (At Airport) - Class A weather station; (Army) Army weather teletype, 24-hr. operation.

TRANSPORTATION:
AIRLINES - None reported.
RAILROADS - Missouri-Kansas-Texas; Missouri Pacific; Southern Pacific; at San Antonio.
Sidings - On field.
ROADS - State No. 218, 1.2 mi. NNW, paved.
FACILITIES - Bus service.

COMMUNICATIONS: Telephone; telegraph; teletype.

PERSONNEL ACCOMMODATIONS (Transient):
At Airport - 150 officers; 150 enlisted men.
In Vicinity - At San Antonio.

Randolph Auxiliary
(Cade Field)

SIZE: 116 acres (total area).
LANDING AREA: All-way field:
N/S 2,095' x E/W 2,420', bare.
APPROACH HAZARDS: None
reported.
HANGARS: None.
SHOPS: None.
GASOLINE:
At Airport - None.
In Vicinity - At Randolph Field.
OIL:
At Airport - None.
In Vicinity - At San Antonio.
RADIO FACILITIES:
RANGE -None.
TOWER - None.
GND/AIR - None.
INSTRUMENT APPROACH
AND LETDOWN
PROCEDURE - None.
WEATHER: (Records from Station
at San Antonio):
PREVAILING WIND-SE,
except Nov., Dec., Jan., N;
Feb., NE.

PRECIPITATION - Av. mo.,
1.34" (Jan.) to 3.24" (Sept.);
av. yr., 27.39".
TEMPERATURE - Av. min. and
max., 58.8° to 79.3°; extremes,
4° to 107°.
FOG - Night.
FACILITIES (At Airport)-
None.
TRANSPORTATION:
AIRLINES - None reported.
RAILROADS - Missouri-
Kansas-Texas; Missouri
Pacific; Southern Pacific; at
San Antoio.
Sidings - At San Antonio.
ROADS - U.S. No. 81, 0.4 mi.
NW; county road,
adjacent N; paved.
FACILITIES - Bus service.
COMMUNICATIONS: None.
PERSONNEL ACCOMMODA-
TIONS (Transient):
At Airport - None.
In Vicinity - At San Antonio.

Randolph Auxiliary (Davenport Field)

U.S. Army Air Force Information Sheets
April 1945 (Formerly Restricted)

SIZE: 208 acres (total area).
LANDING AREA: All-way field:
3,412' x 2,629', sod.
APPROACH HAZARDS: None
HANGARS: None.
SHOPS: None.
GASOLINE:
At Airport - None.
In Vicinity - At Randolph Field.
OIL:
At Airport - None.
In Vicinity - At San Antonio.
RADIO FACILITIES:
RANGE -None.
TOWER - None.
GND/AIR - None.
INSTRUMENT APPROACH
AND LETDOWN
PROCEDURE - None.
WEATHER: (Records from Station
at San Antonio):
PREVAILING WIND-SE,
except Nov., Dec., Jan., N;
Feb., NE.
PRECIPITATION - Av. mo.,

1.34" (Jan.) to 3.24" (Sept.);
av. yr., 27.39".
TEMPERATURE - Av. min. and
max., 58.8° to 79.3°; extremes,
4° to 107°.
FOG - Night.
FACILITIES (At Airport)-
None.
TRANSPORTATION:
AIRLINES - None reported.
RAILROADS - Missouri-
Kansas-Texas; Missouri
Pacific; Southern Pacific; at
San Antoio.
Sidings - 6.0 mi. from field.
ROADS - U.S. No. 81, 1.5 mi.
SE, paved; county road,
adjacent NW, improved.
FACILITIES - Bus service.
COMMUNICATIONS: None.
PERSONNEL ACCOMMODA-
TIONS (Transient):
At Airport - None.
In Vicinity - At San Antonio.

Randolph Auxiliary (Krueger Field)

U.S. Army Air Force Information Sheets
April 1945 (Formerly Restricted)

SIZE: 115 acres (total area).
LANDING AREA: All-way field:
   2,319' x 2,172', bare.
APPROACH HAZARDS: None
HANGARS: None.
SHOPS: None.
GASOLINE:
   At Airport - None.
   In Vicinity - At Randolph Field.
OIL:
   At Airport - None.
   In Vicinity - None.
RADIO FACILITIES:
   RANGE -None.
   TOWER - None.
   GND/AIR - None.
   INSTRUMENT APPROACH
   AND LETDOWN
   PROCEDURE - None.
WEATHER: (Records from Station
   at Seguin):
   PREVAILING WIND-S,
   except Nov., Dec., Jan., N.
   PRECIPITATION - Av. mo.,

1.10" (July) to 4.88" (May);
av. yr., 27.97".
TEMPERATURE - Av. min. and
max., 60.1° to 80°; extremes,
9° to 109°.
FOG - Night.
FACILITIES (At Airport)-
None.
TRANSPORTATION:
AIRLINES - None reported.
RAILROADS - Missouri-
Kansas-Texas; Missouri
Pacific; Southern Pacific; at
San Antoio.
Sidings - At San Antonio.
ROADS - U.S. No. 90, 1.0 mi.
SE, paved; county road,
0.4 mi. ENE, improved.
FACILITIES - None.
COMMUNICATIONS: None.
PERSONNEL ACCOMMODA-
TIONS (Transient):
At Airport - None.
In Vicinity - At San Antonio.

Randolph Auxiliary (Martindale Field)

U.S. Army Air Force Information Sheets
April 1945 (Formerly Restricted)

SIZE: 270 acres (total area).

LANDING AREA: Runways: N/S 3,000' x 400', NW/SE 3,000' x 400', paved.

APPROACH HAZARDS: All approached clear.

HANGARS: None.

SHOPS: None.

GASOLINE:
At Airport - None.
In Vicinity - At Randolph Field.

OIL:
At Airport - None.
In Vicinity - At Randolph Field.

RADIO FACILITIES:
RANGE -None.
TOWER - None.
GND/AIR - None.
INSTRUMENT APPROACH AND LETDOWN PROCEDURE - None.

WEATHER:
PREVAILING WIND-SE, except Nov., Dec., Jan., N. Feb., NE.

PRECIPITATION - Av. mo., 1.34" (Jan.) to 3.24" (Sept.); av. yr., 27.39".

TEMPERATURE - Av. min. and max., 58.8° to 79.3°; extremes, 4° to 107°.

FOG - Night.

FACILITIES (At Airport)- None.

TRANSPORTATION:
AIRLINES - None reported.
RAILROADS - Missouri-Kansas-Texas; Missouri Pacific; Southern Pacific; at San Antoio.
Sidings - At San Antonio.
ROADS - U.S. No. 90, 0.5 mi. NW paved.
FACILITIES - None.

COMMUNICATIONS: None.

PERSONNEL ACCOMMODA-TIONS (Transient):
At Airport - None.
In Vicinity - At San Antonio.

Randolph Auxiliary (Zuehl Field)

U.S. Army Air Force Information Sheets
April 1945 (Formerly Restricted)

SIZE: 280 acres (total area).
LANDING AREA: Runways: N/S 3,000' x 400', NW/SE 3,000' x 400', paved.
APPROACH HAZARDS: None reported.
HANGARS: None.
SHOPS: None.
GASOLINE:
  At Airport - None.
  In Vicinity - At Randolph Field.
OIL:
  At Airport - None.
  In Vicinity - At Randolph Field.
RADIO FACILITIES:
  RANGE -None.
  TOWER - None.
  GND/AIR - None.
  INSTRUMENT APPROACH AND LETDOWN PROCEDURE - None.
WEATHER:
  PREVAILING WIND-S, except Nov., Dec., Jan., N.
  PRECIPITATION - Av. mo.,

1.10" (July) to 4.88" (May); av. yr., 27.97".
TEMPERATURE - Av. min. and max., 60.1° to 80°; extremes, 9° to 109°.
FOG - Night.
FACILITIES (At Airport)- None.
TRANSPORTATION:
  AIRLINES - None reported.
  RAILROADS - Missouri-Kansas-Texas; Missouri Pacific; Southern Pacific; at San Antonio.
  Sidings - At San Antonio.
  ROADS - U.S. No. 90, 1.25 mi. N, paved; county roads adjacent SE and 0.5 mi. W, improved.
  FACILITIES - None.
COMMUNICATIONS: None.
PERSONNEL ACCOMMODA-TIONS (Transient):
  At Airport - None.
  In Vicinity - At San Antonio.

Waco Army Air Field
Waco

SIZE: 1,364 acres.

LANDING AREA: Runways: N/S 6,314' x 150', N/S 4,783' x 150', NE/SW 5,500' x 150', NW/SE 5,632' x 150', NW/SE 4,283' x 150', concrete.

APPROACH HAZARDS: 45' trees, SW.

HANGARS: (1) 184' x 100', door 100' x 20', steel and metal.

SHOPS: Major repairs.

GASOLINE:
At Airport - 73, 87, and 100 octane, 187,000 gal.; tank capacity, 262,000 gal.; 10 servicing trucks, total capacity, 20,000 gal.
In Vicinity - At Waco.

OIL:
At Airport - SAE 1120, 100,000 qt., in underground storage.
In Vicinity - At Waco.

RADIO FACILITIES:
RANGE -None.
TOWER - 396 kcs.; continuous.
INSTRUMENT APPROACH AND LETDOWN PROCEDURE - None.

WEATHER:
PREVAILING WIND-S, except Nov., Dec., Jan., Feb., N.
PRECIPITATION - Av. mo., 2.01" (Jan.) to 4.59" (May); av. yr., 35.26".
TEMPERATURE - Av. min. and max., 57.1° to 78.3°; extremes, -5° to 109°.
FOG - Spring and fall.
FACILITIES - First-order weather station.

TRANSPORTATION:
AIRLINES - None reported.
RAILROADS - Missouri-Kansas-Texas; Missouri Pacific; St. Louis Southwestern; Southern Pacific; at Waco. Sidings - On field.
ROADS - U.S. Nos. 77 and 81, 1.9 mi. W, paved; county roads, adjacent N and adjacent S, improved.
FACILITIES - Bus and taxi.

COMMUNICATIONS: Telephone; telegraph; teletype.

PERSONNEL ACCOMMODATIONS :
At Airport - 100 officers; 1,500 enlisted men.
In Vicinity - At Waco.

Photographs and specifications of the principal training and operational aircraft flown from the eight army airfields featured in this book.

— All photo information courtesy U.S. Air Force Museum —

Boeing B-17G "Flying Fortress"

The Flying Fortress is one of the most famous airplanes ever built. The B-17 prototype first flew on July 28, 1935. Few B-17s were in service on December 7, 1941, but production quickly accelerated. The aircraft served in every WW II combat zone, but is best known for daylight strategic bombing of German industrial targets. Production ended in May 1945 and totaled 12,726.

In March 1944 this B-17G was assigned to the 91st Bomb Group—"The Ragged Irregulars"—and based at Bassingbourn, England. There it was named *Shoo Shoo Baby* by its crew, after a popular song. It flew 24 combat missions in WWII, receiving flak damage seven times. Its first mission (Frankfurt, Germany) was on March 24, 1944, and last mission (Posen, Poland) on May 29, 1944, when engine problems forced a landing in neutral Sweden where the airplane and crew were interned. In 1968, *Shoo Shoo Baby* was found abandoned in France; the French government presented the airplane to the USAF. In July 1978, the 512th Military Airlift Wing moved it to Dover AFB, Delaware, for restoration by the volunteers of the 512th Antique Restoration Group. The massive ten-year job of restoration to flying condition was completed in 1988 and the aircraft was flown to the Museum in October 1988.

SPECIFICATIONS
Span: 103 ft. 10 in.
Length: 74 ft. 4 in.
Height: 19 ft. 1 in.
Weight: 55,000 lbs. loaded
Armament: Thirteen .50-cal. machine guns with normal bomb load of 6,000 lbs.
Engines: Four Wright "Cyclone" R-1820s of 1,200 hp. ea.
Cost: $276,000
Serial Number: 42-32076
PERFORMANCE
Maximum speed: 300 mph.
Cruising speed: 170 mph.
Range: 1,850 miles
Service Ceiling: 35,000 ft.

Boeing B-29 "Superfortress"

The Boeing B-29 was designed in 1940 as an eventual replacement for the B-17 and B-24. The first one built made its maiden flight on September 21, 1942. In December 1943 it was decided not to use the B-29 in the European Theater, thereby permitting the airplane to be sent to the Pacific area where its great range made it particularly suited for the long overwater flight required to attack the Japanese homeland from bases in China. During the last two months of 1944, B-29s began operating against Japan from the islands of Saipan, Guam, and Tinian.

With the advent of the conflict in Korea in June 1950, the B-29 was once again thrust into battle. For the next several years it was effectively used for attacking targets in North Korea.

The B-29 on display, named "*Bockscar*," was flown to the U.S. Air Force Museum on September 26, 1961. It is the airplane from which the second atomic bomb was dropped on Nagasaki on August 9, 1945.

SPECIFICATIONS
Span: 141 ft. 3 in.
Length: 99 ft. 0 in.
Height: 27 ft. 9 in.
Weight: 133,500 lbs. max.
Armament: Eight .50-cal. machine guns in remote controlled turrets plus two .50-cal. machine guns and one 20mm cannon in tail; 20,000 lbs. of bombs
Engines: Four Wright R-3350s of 2,200 hp. ea.
Cost: $639,000
Serial Number: 44-27297
PERFORMANCE
Maximum speed: 357 mph.
Cruising speed: 220 mph.
Range: 3,700 miles
Service Ceiling: 33,600 ft.

Cessna UC-78B "Bobcat"

The UC-78 is a military version of the commercial Cessna T-50 light transport. Cessna first produced the wood and tubular steel, fabric covered T-50 in 1939 for the civilian market. In 1940, the Air Corps ordered them under the designation AT-8 as multi-engine advanced trainers.

Thirty-three AT-8s were built for the Air Corps, and production continued under the designation AT-17 reflecting a change in equipment and engine types. In 1942, the AAF adopted the Bobcat as a light personnel transport and those delivered after January 1, 1943, were designated UC-78s. By the end of WW II, Cessna had produced more than 4,600 Bobcats for the AAF, 67 of which were transferred to the U.S. Navy as JRC-1s. In addition, 822 Bobcats had been produced for the Royal Canadian Air Force as Crane 1s.

Dubbed the "Bamboo Bomber" by the pilots who flew them, it was one of the aircraft featured in the popular television series "Sky King" of the 1940s and 1950s.

The UC-78 on display is one of the 1,806-Bs built for the AAF. It was acquired by the Museum in 1982.

SPECIFICATIONS
    Span: 41 ft. 11 in.
    Length: 32 ft. 9 in.
    Height: 9 ft. 11 in.
    Weight: 5,700 lbs. max.
    Armament: None
    Engines: Two Jacobs R-755-9s of 245 hp. each
    Cost: $31,000
    Serial Number: 42-71626
    C/N: 4322
    Other Registrations: N43BB, N4403N
PERFORMANCE
    Maximum speed: 175 mph.
    Cruising speed: 150 mph.
    Range: 750 miles
    Service Ceiling: 15,000 ft.

This aircraft is awaiting restoration

Consolidated B-24D "Liberator"

The B-24 was employed in operations in every combat theater during the war. Because of its great range, it was particularly suited for such missions as the famous raid from North Africa against the oil industry at Ploesti, Rumania, on August 1, 1943. This feature also made the airplane suitable for long over-water missions in the Pacific Theater. More than 18,000 Liberators were produced.

The B-24D on display flew combat missions from North Africa in 1943-1944 with the 512th Bomb Squadron. It was flown to the U.S. Air Force Museum in May 1959. It is the same type airplane as the *Lady Be Good*, the world-famous B-24D which disappeared on a mission from North Africa in April 1943 and which was found in the Libyan Desert in May 1959.

SPECIFICATIONS
> Span: 110 ft. 0 in.
> Length: 66 ft. 4 in.
> Height: 17 ft. 11 in.
> Weight: 56,000 lbs. loaded
> Armament: Ten .50-cal. machine guns and 8,000 lbs. of bombs
> Engines: Four Pratt & Whitney R-1830s of 1,200 hp. ea.
> Cost: $336,000
> Serial Number: 42-72843

PERFORMANCE
> Maximum speed: 303 mph.
> Cruising speed: 175 mph.
> Range: 2,850 mph.
> Service Ceiling: 28,000 ft.

Consolidated PT-1 "Trusty"

The PT-1, produced by the Air Service in 1925, established the basic design for primary trainers into the World War II period. It was also the first airplane purchased in substantial quantity following World War I, with 221 being delivered from production. It was used extensively during the late 1920s and early 1930s for training avaition cadets in California and Texas.

Developed from the Dayton-Wright TW-3 airplane, the PT-1 featured an innovation for trainers, a welded fuselage framework of chrome-molybdenum steel tubing for providing greater structural strength. The airplane was so sturdy and dependable that it was nicknamed the "Trusty." However, it was so easy to fly that it bred overconfidence in some who were soon to be flying faster airplanes having more difficult handling characteristics.

The airplane on display was obtained from the Ohio State University in 1957.

SPECIFICATIONS
   Span: 34 ft. 9 1/2 in.
   Length: 27 ft. 8 in.
   Height: 9 ft. 6 in.
   Weight: 2,550 lbs. loaded
   Armament: None
   Engine: Wright "E" of 180 hp. (Hispano-Suiza design)
   Cost: $8,000

PERFORMANCE
  Maximum speed: 99 mph.
  Cruising speed: 78 mph.
  Range: 310 miles
  Service Ceiling: 13,450 ft.

Curtiss P-40E "Warhawk"

The P-40, developed from the P-36, was America's foremost fighter in service when WWII began. P-40s engaged Japanese aircraft during the attack on Pearl Harbor and the invasion of the Philippines in December 1941. They also were flown in China early in 1942 by the famed Flying Tigers and in North Africa in 1943 by the first AAF all-black unit, the 99th Fighter Squadron.

The P-40 served in numerous combat areas—the Aleutian Islands, Italy, the Middle East, the Far East, the Southwest Pacific, and some were sent to Russia. Though often outclassed by its adversaries in speed, maneuverability and rate of climb, the P-40 earned a reputation in battle for extreme ruggedness. At the end of the P-40's brilliant career, more than 14,000 had been produced for service in the air forces of 28 nations, of which 2,320 were of the "E" series.

The airplane on display, a "Kittyhawk" (the export version of the P-40E built for the RAF), was obtained from Mr. Charles P. Doyle, Rosemount, Minnesota. It is painted as the P-40E flown in combat by Bruce Holloway, a pilot in both the Flying Tigers and its successor AAF unit, the 23rd Fighter Group. During his tour in China, Colonel Holloway, who retired as a four star general in 1972 while the commander of the

Strategic Air Command (SAC), had a total of thirteen Japanese planes to his credit.

SPECIFICATIONS
Span: 37 ft. 4 in.
Length: 31 ft. 9 in.
Height: 12 ft. 4 in.
Weight: 9,100 lbs. loaded
Armament: Six .50-cal. machine guns; 700 lbs. of bombs externally.
Engine: Allison V-1710 of 1,150 hp.
Cost: $45,000
PERFORMANCE
Maximum speed: 362 mph.
Cruising speed: 235 mph.
Range: 850 miles
Service Ceiling: 30,000 ft.

Fairchild PT-19A "Cornell"

The PT-19 developed by Fairchild in 1938 to satisfy a military requirement for a rugged monoplane primary trainer, was ordered into quantity production in 1940. In addition to being manufactured by Fairchild during WWII, the "Cornell" was produced in the U.S. by the Aeronca, Howard, and St. Louis Aircraft Corporations and in Canada by Fleet Aircraft, Ltd.

Some Cornells were powered by Continental radial engines and designated PT-23s, while others were produced with cockpit canopies and designated PT-26s. Altogether, 7,742 Cornells were manufactured for the AAF, with 4,889 of them being PT-19s. Additional Cornells were supplied to Canada, Norway, Brazil, Ecuador, and Chile.

The PT-19A on display was donated to the Air Force Museum in November 1984 by Mr. Howard Phillips, Seattle, Washington.

SPECIFICATIONS
Span: 35 ft. 11 3/16 in.
Length: 27 ft. 8 3/8 in.
Height: 7 ft. 9 in.
Weight: 2,450 lbs. loaded
Armament: None
Engine: Ranger L-440 of 175 hp.
PERFORMANCE
Maximum speed: 124 mph.
Cruising speed: 106 mph.
Range: 480 miles
Service Ceiling: 16,000 ft.

North American T-6G "Texan"

The AT-6 advanced trainer was one of the most widely used aircraft in history. Evolving from the BC-1 basic combat trainer ordered in 1937, 15,495 Texans were built between 1938 and 1945. The USAAF procured 10,057 AT-6s; others went to the Navy as SNJs and to more than 30 Allied nations. Most AAF fighter pilots trained in AT-6s prior to graduation from flying school. Many of the "Spitfire" and "Hurricane" pilots in the Battle of Britain trained in Canada in "Harvards," the British version of the AT-6. To comply with neutrality laws, U.S. built Harvards were flown north to the border and were pushed across.

In 1948, Texans still in USAF service were redesignated as T-6s when the AT, BT, and PT aircraft designations were abandoned. To meet an urgent need for close air support of ground forces in the Korean Conflict, T-6s flew "mosquito missions" spotting enemy troops and guns and marking them with smoke rockets for attack by fighter-bombers.

The aircraft on display is one of 1,802 T-6s remanufactured under a 1949 USAF modernization program, redesignated as T-6Gs, and given new serial numbers. It was acquired from the Pennsylvania Air National Guard in 1957 and is painted as an AT-6 based at Randolph Field, Texas, in 1942.

SPECIFICATIONS
> Span: 42 ft.
> Length: 29 ft. 6 in.
> Height: 10 ft. 10 in.
> Weight: 5,617 lbs. loaded.
> Armament: None (some AT-6s used for gunnery/bombing
training).
> Engine: Pratt & Whitney R-1340 of 600 hp.
> Cost: $27,000

PERFORMANCE
> Maximum speed: 210 mph.
> Cruising speed: 145 mph.
> Range: 770 miles.
> Service Ceiling: 23,200 ft.

Republic P-47D "Thunderbolt"

The P-47 was one of America's leading fighter airplanes of WW II. It made its initial flight on May 6, 1941, but the first production article was not delivered to the AAF until March 18, 1942, more than three months after the attack on Pearl Harbor. On April 8, 1943, the P-47 flew its first combat mission, taking off from England for a sweep over western Europe. During the next several months, AAF pilots learned that the Thunderbolt could out-dive any Luftwaffe airplane encountered. An auxilary fuel tank was suspended under the fuselage beginning in 1943, permitting the P-47 to escort AAF heavy bombers much farther into German territory.

In addition to establishing an impressive record as a high-altitude escort fighter, the P-47 gained recognition as a low-level fighter-bomber because of its ability to absorb battle damage and keep flying. By the end of the war, the Thunderbolt had been used in every active war theater with the exception of Alaska. In addition to serving with the AAF, some were flown in action by the British, Free French, Russians, Mexicans, and Brazilians.

The P-47D on display, one of more than 15,600 built, was donated by Republic Aviation Corporation in November 1964.

SPECIFICATIONS
    Span: 40 ft. 9 in.
    Length: 36 ft. 1 in.
    Height: 14 ft. 2 in.
    Weight: 13,500 lbs. loaded

Armament: Eight .50-cal. machine guns and ten 5 in. rockets or 1,500 lbs. of bombs.
Engine: Pratt and Whitney R-2800 of 2,300 hp.
Serial number: 42-23278

PERFORMANCE
Maximum speed: 433 mph
Cruising speed: 260 mph
Range: 1,100 miles (with auxiliary fuel tank)
Service Ceiling: 40,000 ft.

Vultee BT-13B "Valiant"

As temporarily displayed in the Annex.

The "Valiant" was the basic trainer most widely used by the USAAF during WW II. It represented the second of the three stages of pilot training—primary, basic, and advanced. Compared with the primary trainers in use at the time, it was considerably more complex. The BT-13 not only had a more powerful engine, it was also faster and heavier. In addition, it required the student pilot to use two-way radio communications with the ground, operate landing flaps and a two-position variable pitch propeller.

Nicknamed the "Vibrator" by the pilots who flew it, the BT-13 was powered by a Pratt & Whitney R-985 engine. But to counter the shortage of these engines early in the BT-13 production program, 1,693 Valiants were produced in 1941-1942 with a Wright R-975 engine and were designated as BT-15s. By the end of WW II, 10,375 BT-13s and BT-15s had been accepted by the AAF.

The BT-13 on display, one of 1,775 -Bs built, was acquired from Mr. Raymond Brandly of West Carrollton, Ohio, in 1965.

SPECIFICATIONS
    Span: 42 ft. 2 in.
    Length: 28 ft. 8½ in.
    Height: 12 ft. 4¾ in.
    Weight: 4,227 lbs. loaded
    Armament: None
    Engine: Pratt & Whitney R-985 of 450 hp.
    Crew: Two (instructor & student)
    Cost: $20,000
    Serial number: 42-90629
PERFORMANCE
    Maximum speed: 155 mph.
    Cruising speed: 130 mph.
    Range: 880 miles
    Service Ceiling: 19,400 ft.

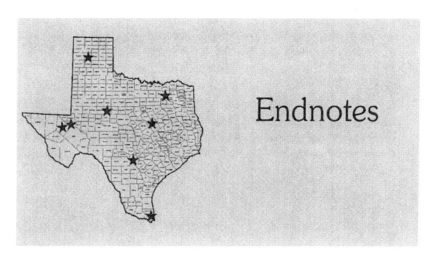

Endnotes

NOTES TO CHAPTER I
1. Zane Grey, *West of the Pecos*, 36.
2. John Steinbeck, *Travels With Charley*, 143.
3. *Texas Almanac and State Industrial Guide, 1939-1940*, 93.
4. Pedro de Castañeda de Nájera, *Relacion de la Jornada de Cibola*.
5. Randolph B. Marcy, *The Prairie Traveler*, 94.
6. J. Frank Davis, *Randolph Field: A History and Guide*, 2.
7. *Texas Almanac*, 90.
8. Ibid., 316.
9. Ibid., 253.
10. Ibid., 334.
11. *San Antonio Express*, January 1, 1947.
12. *Texas Almanac*, 87.
13. Ron Tyler, ed., *The New Handbook of Texas*, vol. 6, 1079.
14. Arnold Frank Simpson, interview with author, Abilene, Texas, June 9, 1998.
15. *San Antonio Light*, December 8, 1946.

NOTES TO CHAPTER II
1. Richard E. Gilliam, telephone interview with author, May 9, 1998.
2. Orrin Mc. Huffman, "My Life on the Run," *Fort Worth Star-Telegram*, June 12, 1933.
3. Ron Tyler, ed., *The New Handbook of Texas*, vol. 5, 119.
4. Bill Davenport, interview with author, Pecos, Texas, October 3, 1998.
5. *Pecos Enterprise*, September 11, 1942.
6. Tyler, ed., vol. 5, 119.
7. *Pecos Army Air Field 1998 Reunion Booklet*, 23.
8. *Pecos Enterprise*, December 19, 1941.

9. *Reunion Booklet,* 23.

10. *Texas Almanac and State Industrial Guide,* 1939-1940, 448.

11. West of Pecos Museum volunteer, interview with author, October 3, 1998. (Anonymity requested).

12. *Reunion Booklet,* 23.

13. *Pecos Enterprise,* October 8, 1998.

14. Lucy Rountree Kuykendall, *P.S. to Pecos,* xi.

15. *Pecos Enterprise,* October 8, 1998.

16. Tyler, ed., vol. 5, 120.

17. *Reunion Booklet,* 24.

18. Kuykendall, 103.

19. Tyler, ed., vol. 5, 119.

20. Kuykendall, 249.

21. Ibid., xi.

22. Ibid., 81.

23. Ibid., 124.

24. Bill Pitts, interview with author, Pecos, Texas, October 4, 1998.

25. Kuykendall, 249-250.

26. *Reunion Booklet,* 24.

27. Tyler, ed., vol. 5, 120.

28. Davenport interview.

29. Stan Brown, interview with author, Pecos, Texas, October 2, 1998.

30. James Turner, comments at 1998 Reunion session, Pecos, Texas, October 3, 1998.

31. L. M. McDonald, *Reunion Booklet,* 7.

32. Ibid., 7.

33. Leslie Kleeb, comments at 1998 Reunion session, Pecos, Texas, October 3, 1998.

34. Davenport interview.

35. Kuykendall, 257.

NOTES TO CHAPTER III

1. Alvin M. Josephy, ed., *The American Heritage History of Flight,* 144-145.

2. *Sweetwater Reporter,* June 28, 1942.

3. Bennet B. Monde, *Wings Over Sweetwater: The History of Avenger Field,* 10.

4. Ibid., 31.

5. *Sweetwater Reporter,* August 15, 1942.

6. Ibid., June 28, 1942.

7. Ibid.

8. Erskine J. Lloyd, letter to author, July 30, 1998.

9. Melvin A. Lassiter, telephone interview with author, August 16, 1998.

10. E. L. Yeats and Hooper Shelton, *History of Nolan County, Texas,* 106.

11. Emily Turner Cole, interview with author, Abilene, Texas, July 28, 1998.

12. Monde, 33.

13. Sally Van Wagenen Keil, *Those Wonderful Women in Their Flying Machines,* 107.

14. Yeats and Shelton, 106.

15. Janet Daily, *Silver Wings/Santiago Blue*, 109.

16. Jean Hascall Cole, *Women Pilots of World War II*, 3.

17. *Avenger*, May 11, 1943.

18. Jacqueline Cochran, *The Stars at Noon*, 197.

19. Mary Beth Rogers, Sherry A. Smith and Janelle D. Scott, *We Can Fly: Stories of Katherine Stinson and Other Gutsy Texas Women Pilots*, 149.

20. Sheilah Henderson, "Zoot Suits, Parachutes, and Wings of Silver, Too," *Texas Highways*, September 1987, 10.

21. Louise Bradford, "A History of Nolan County, Texas," (master's thesis, University of Texas, 1934) 12.

22. Doris Brinker Tanner, comp., *Who Were the WASP?*, 42.

23. Keil, 160.

24. Ibid., 380.

25. Cochran, 220.

26. Keil, 163.

27. *Avenger*, August 12, 1943.

28. Keil, 181.

29. Byrd Howell Granger, *On Final Approach*, 240.

30. Delpha Lawrence, letter to author, September 11, 1998.

31. Addie Harrison, telephone interview with author, August 30, 1998.

32. Marianne Verges, *On Silver Wings, 1942-44: The Women Airforce Service Pilots of World War II*, 83.

33. Keil, 277.

34. *Avenger*, March 17, 1944.

35. Keil, 4.

36. Ibid., 282.

37. *Avenger*, July 14, 1944.

38. Rogers and others, 151.

39. Keil, 327.

40. Monde, 78.

41. *Sweetwater Reporter*, May 21, 1993.

NOTES TO CHAPTER IV

1. Pedro de Castañeda de Nájera, *Relacion de la Jornada de Cibola*.

2. Ron Tyler, ed., *New Handbook of Texas*, vol. 1, 140.

3. Ibid., 141.

4. The highway distance from Amarillo to Santa Fe, New Mexico, is 280 miles, and it is 424 miles to Colorado's state capital at Denver. From Amarillo to Oklahoma City is 259 miles while Austin, Texas, is 497 miles away.

5. *Amarillo Daily News*, December 12, 1927.

6. *Amarillo News-Globe*, September 10, 1941.

7. Ibid.

8. Ibid.

9. Ibid.

10. *Amarillo Daily News*, November 29, 1941.

11. Ibid.

12. Wesley W. Jones and Joe D. LaCrone, "History of Amarillo Air Force Base," 1.

13. *Amarillo News-Globe*, September 27, 1942.

14. Ibid.

15. *Amarillo Daily News*, May 27, 1942.

16. *Amarillo News-Globe*, March 21, 1944.

17. Jones and LaCrone, 6.

18. Ibid., 8.

19. Ibid., 12.

20. *Amarillo News-Globe*, October 25, 1967.

NOTES TO CHAPTER V

1. *Texas Almanac and State Industrial Guide*, 1939-1940, 426.

2. *Greenville Evening Banner*, October 7, 1998.

3. Ron Tyler, ed., *The New Handbook of Texas*, vol. 3, 785.

4. Ibid., 785.

5. Ibid., vol. 1, 47.

6. Ibid., vol. 4, 347.

7. W. Walworth Harrison, *History of Greenville and Hunt County*, 387.

8. Tyler, ed., vol. 3, 785.

9. *Greenville Evening Banner*, January 6, 1942.

10. Harrison, 345.

11. Fred H. Allison, "Majors Field and Greenville, Texas in World War II," (master's thesis, East Texas State University, 1995), 27.

12. W. A. Caplinder and Jim Conrad, "A History of Majors Airfield, Greenville, Texas," 7.

13. Allison, 37.

14. *Greenville Evening Banner*, January 4, 1943.

15. Allison, 127.

16. Ibid., 123.

17. Ibid., 154.

18. John Bollow, "Remembering the WASPS," *The Saturday Evening Post*, May/June 1995.

19. W. A. Caplinder, interview with author, Greenville, Texas, October 15, 1998.

20. Ibid.

21. Allison, 21.

22. Ibid., 83.

23. Vincent Leibowitz, interview with author, Greenville, Texas, October 15, 1998.

24. Gordon Swanborough and Peter M. Bowers, *United States Military Aircraft Since 1909*, 583.

25. William G. Tudor, "Flight of Eagles: The Mexican Expeditionary Air Force 'Escuadron' 201 in World War II," (Ph.D. diss., Texas Christian University, 1997), 2.

26. Ibid., 31.

27. Jose E. Alvarez, "Aguilas Aztecas: The Mexican Air Force During World

War II" (paper presented at the annual meeting of the Texas State Historical Association, Austin, Texas, March 3, 1998), 9.

28. Fred H. Allison, "The Fighting Eagles: Mexico's Squadron 201 in World War II Texas" (paper presented at the annual meeting of the Texas State Historical Association, Austin, Texas, March 3, 1998), 4.

29. Ibid., 4.

30. Tudor, 287.

31. Harrison, 387.

NOTES TO CHAPTER VI

1. Richard J. Veit, ed., "Waco Goes to War," *Waco Heritage and History,* 110.

2. "City of Waco Salutes James Connally Air Force Base," 6.

3. "Guide to James Connally Air Force Base," 5.

4. Jean B. Pitner, "Project of the Community of Waco Air Force Base," 11.

5. Veit, 13.

6. Ibid., 11.

7. Ibid., 32.

8. Patricia Ward Wallace, "Our Land, Our Lives: A Pictorial History of McLennan County," 176.

9. Ron Tyler, ed., *The New Handbook of Texas,* vol. 6, 778.

10. "City of Waco," 8.

11. John R. Wheatley, "The Economic Impact of the Closing of James Connally Air Force Base on the Waco Area," (master's thesis, Baylor University, 1966), 181.

12. Ibid., 51.

13. Ibid., 53.

14. *Waco News Tribune,* March 4, 1965.

15. Ibid., June 9, 1966.

NOTES TO CHAPTER VII

1. Ron Tyler, ed., *The New Handbook of Texas,* vol. 5, 796.

2. *Texas Almanac and State Industrial Guide, 1943-1944,* 86.

3. Eldon S. Cagle, *Quadrangle: The History of Fort Sam Houston,* 30.

4. Ibid., 67.

5. Roger Bilstein and Jay Miller, *Aviation in Texas,* 17.

6. Alfred Goldberg, ed., *A History of the United States Air Force, 1907-1957,* 66.

7. Bilstein and Miller, 18.

8. Cagle, 94.

9. *Texas Almanac,* 86-87.

10. Rossi L. Selvaggi, "A History of Randolph Air Force Base," (master's thesis, University of Texas, 1958), 12.

11. Ibid., 11.

12. Ibid., 13.

13. Thomas Manning, Pat Parrish, and Dick Emmons, "Randolph Field," *A History of Military Aviation in San Antonio,* 75.

14. Ibid., 75.

15. Selvaggi, 21.
16. "Randolph Field," 76.
17. Ibid., 76.
18. Selvaggi, 29.
19. "Randolph Field," 77-78.
20. Selvaggi, 33.
21. "Randolph Field," 80.
22. Ibid., 79-80.
23. Selvaggi, 39.
24. Ibid., 60.
25. Ibid., 68.
26. *San Antonio Light,* June 20, 1930.
27. Selvaggi, 72.
28. Ellen Randolph, "Randolph Field, The West Point of the Air," (unpublished essay, 1930), 8.
29. *San Antonio Light,* June 21, 1930.
30. *San Antonio Express,* June 20, 1930.
31. "Randolph Field," 82.
32. Everett G. Wallace, interview with author, San Antonio, Texas, December 17, 1998.
33. Selvaggi, 103.
34. Ibid., 166.
35. J. Frank Davis, *Randolph Field: A History and Guide,* 84.
36. Ibid., 85.
37. Ibid., 85.
38. *San Antonio Light,* October 13, 1942.
39. Mary Ann Noonan Guerra, *The Gunter Hotel in San Antonio's History,* 30.
40. Davis, 85.
41. Selvaggi, 124.
42. Ibid., 108.
43. Selvaggi, 124.
44. *Texas Almanac,* 1939-1940, 86.
45. *San Antonio Express News,* September 8, 1994.
46. "USAF Almanac, 1998," *Air Force Magazine,* 81, no. 5, May 1998, 123.

NOTES TO CHAPTER VIII
1. Ron Tyler, ed., *The New Handbook of Texas,* vol. 3, 463.
2. "Meteorological Facts," *Harlingen Chamber of Commerce Bulletin,* 3.
3. Vance Delone Raimond, *Transportation: Key to the Magic Valley,* 134.
4. *Valley Morning Star,* February 1, 1941.
5. Raimond, 135.
6. *Valley Morning Star,* June 20, 1963.
7. Ibid., July 30, 1944.
8. *Welcome to Harlingen,* 2.
9. Raimond, 137.
10. Doris Brinker Tanner, *Who Were the WASP?,* 101.
11. *New York Daily News,* June 25, 1943.

12. *Chicago Tribune,* June 26, 1943.
13. Charlotte Meade Blankenship, interview with author, Brownsville, Texas, October 28, 1998.
14. *Harlingen Valley Times,* April 17, 1961.
15. *Valley Morning Star,* November 12, 1960.
16. Thomas K. Radley, interview with author, Harlingen, Texas, October 28, 1998.
17. Raimond, 142.
18. *Valley Morning Star,* July 30, 1964.
19. *Corpus Christi Caller Times,* April 4, 1965.
20. Ibid.
21. *Valley Morning Star,* August 12, 1997.

NOTES TO CHAPTER IX
1. Ron Tyler, ed., *The New Handbook of Texas,* vol. 5, 374.
2. Ibid., 374.
3. *Texas Almanac and State Industrial Guide, 1939-1940,* 88.
4. Ibid., 88.
5. Tyler, ed., vol. 5, 374.
6. Elizabeth Heath, comp., *Ward County 1887-1977,* 222.
7. *Monahans News,* July 24, 1942.
8. Ibid., July 31, 1942.
9. *Texas Almanac,* 460.
10. Daniel M. Selph, interview with author, October 4, 1998.
11. Ibid.
12. *San Angelo Standard-Times,* February 16, 1954.
13. Heath, comp., 222.
14. *San Antonio Express,* July 29, 1976.
15. *Monahans News,* July 21, 1944.
16. Heath, comp., 222.
17. *Monahans News,* January 15, 1943.
18. Ibid.
19. Ibid., January 5, 1945.
20. Ibid., August 4, 1944.
21. Heath, comp., 230.
22. *Monahans News,* July 15, 1976.
23. Ibid.
24. Heath, comp., 235.
25. Ibid., 224.

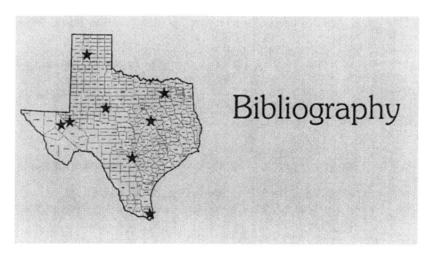

Bibliography

Allison, Fred H. "Majors Field and Greenville, Texas, in World War II." Master's thesis, East Texas State University, 1995.

———."The Fighting Eagles: Mexico's Squadron 201 in World War II Texas." Paper presented at the annual meeting of the Texas State Historical Association, Austin, Texas, March 3, 1998.

Altman, Harlan F. Interview with author. San Benito, Texas. October 29, 1998.

Alvarez, Jose E. "Aguilas Aztecas: The Mexican Air Force During World War II." Paper presented at the annual meeting of the Texas State Historical Association, Austin, Texas, March 3, 1998.

Amarillo Daily News: December 12, 1927; November 29, 1941; May 27, 1942.

Amarillo News-Globe: September 10, 1941; April 2, 1942; September 27, 1942; March 21, 1944; October 25, 1967.

Avenger: May 11, 1943; August 12, 1943; March 17, 1944; July 14, 1944.

Belcher, George F. Interview with author. Fort Worth, Texas. December 2, 1998.

Bilstein, Roger and Jay Miller. *Aviation In Texas.* Austin: Texas Monthly Press, 1985.

Blankenship, Charlotte Meade. Interview with author. Brownsville, Texas. October 28, 1998.

Bollow, John. "Remembering the WASPS." *The Saturday Evening Post* (May/June 1995).

Bradford, Louise. "A History of Nolan County, Texas," Master's thesis, University of Texas, 1934.

Bright, Charles D., ed. *Historical Dictionary of the United States Air Force.* New York: Greenwood Press, 1992.

Brownlee, Marian Harris. Interview with author. Commerce, Texas. October 15, 1998.

Brownsville Herald, January 1, 1986.

249

Cagle, Eldon, Jr. *Quadrangle: The History of Fort Sam Houston.* Austin: Eakin Press, 1985.
Caplinder, W. A. Interview with author. Greenville, Texas. October 14, 1998.
———, and Jim Conrad. *A History of Majors Air Field, Greenville, Texas.* Greenville: Hunt County Historical Commission, 1994.
Castañeda de Nájera, Pedro de. *Relacion de la Jornada de Cibola.* Microfilm no. 63, Rich Collection. New York Public Library, New York City.
Chicago Tribune, June 23, 1943.
City of Waco Salutes James Connally Air Force Base. Washington, D.C.: Armed Guide Directory Publishers, 1962.
Cochran, Jacqueline. *The Stars at Noon.* Boston: Little, Brown and Company, 1954.
Cole, Emily Turner. Interview with author. Abilene, Texas. June 9, 1998.
Cole, Jean Hascall. *Women Pilots of World War II.* Salt Lake City: University of Utah Press, 1971.
Corpus Christi Caller-Times, April 4, 1965.
Crane, Abel David. Interview with author. Snyder, Texas. June 11, 1998.
Craven, Wesley Frank and James Lea Cate. *The Army Air Forces in World War II.* Washington, D.C.: Office of Air Force History, 1983.
Daily, Janet. *Silver Wings/Santiago Blue.* New York: Poseidon Press, 1984.
Davenport, Bill. Interview with author. Pecos, Texas. October 3, 1998.
Davis, J. Frank. *Randolph Field: A History and Guide.* New York: The Devin-Adair Company, 1942.
Fogerty, Robert P. *Biographical Data on Air Force General Officers, 1917-1952.* USAF Historical Study 91. Maxwell Air Force Base (ALA): USAF Historical Division, Air University, 1953.
Fort Worth Star-Telegram, June 12, 1933.
Frisbee, John L., ed. *Makers of the United States Air Force.* Washington, D.C.: Office of Air Force History, 1987.
Gilliam, Richard E. Telephone interview with author. May 6, 1998.
Goldberg, Alfred, ed. *A History of the United States Air Force, 1907-1957.* Princeton, (N.J.): Van Nostrand, 1957.
Gott, Kay. *Women in Pursuit.* McKinleyville, (CA): Privately published, 1993.
Granger, Byrd Howell. *On Final Approach.* Scottsdale (AZ): Falconer Publishing Co., 1991.
Granger, Walter M. Interview with author, Waco, Texas. October 17, 1998.
Greenville Evening Banner: January 6, 1942; January 4, 1943; October 7, 1998.
Grey, Zane. *West of the Pecos.* Roslyn (NY): Walter J. Black, Inc., 1931.
Guerra, Mary Ann Noonan. *The Gunter Hotel in San Antonio's History.* San Antonio: The Gunter Hotel, 1985.
Guide to James Connally Air Force Base. Dallas: The Tyndall Press, 1962.
Harlingen Press, April 7, 1961.
Harrison, Addie. Interview with author. Abilene, Texas. June 8, 1998.
Harrison, W. Walworth. *History of Greenville and Hunt County, Texas.* Waco (TX): Texian Press, 1977.
Heath, Elizabeth, comp. *Ward County 1887-1977.* Monahans (TX): Ward County Historical Commission, 1977.

Henderson, Sheilah. "Zoot Suits, Parachutes And Wings Of Silver, Too." *Texas Highways*. Vol. 34, No. 9. (September 1987).

Hennigan, J. R. Interview with author. Odessa, Texas. August 12, 1998.

Jones, Wesley W. and Joe D. LeCrone. "History of Amarillo Air Force Base." Unpublished essay, 1968.

Keil, Sally Van Wagenen. *Those Wonderful Women in Their Flying Machines*. New York: Four Directions Press, 1990.

Kuykendall, Lucy Rountree. *P.S. to Pecos*. Houston: The Anson Jones Press, 1945.

Lassiter, Melvin A. Telephone interview with author. August 16, 1998.

Lawrence, Delpha. Letter to author. September 11, 1998.

Leibowitz, Vincent. Interview with author. Greenville, Texas. October 14, 1998.

Lloyd, Erskine J. Letter to author. July 30, 1998.

Manning, Thomas, Pat Parrish, and Dick Emmons. "Randolph Field." *A History of Military Aviation in San Antonio*. Randolph Air Force Base: History Office, Air Education and Training Command. 1996.

Marcy, Randolph B. *The Prairie Traveler*. Reprint, Old Saybrook (CT): The Globe Pequot Press, 1989.

"Meteorological Facts." Harlingen, Texas, Chamber of Commerce Bulletin, 1940.

McKee, Millicent Bond. Interview with author. Abilene, Texas. June 9, 1998.

Monahans News: July 24, 1942; July 31, 1942; July 21, 1944; January 15, 1943; August 4, 1944; January 5, 1945; July 15, 1976.

Monde, Bennet B. *Wings Over Sweetwater: The History of Avenger Field*. Sweetwater (TX): Privately published, 1995.

New York Daily News, June 25, 1943.

Noggle, Anne. *For God, Country and the Thrill of It All: Women Airforce Service Pilots In World War II*. College Station: Texas A&M University Press, 1990.

Official Guide to the Army Air Forces. New York: Simon and Schuester, 1944.

Overman, Martin. Interview with author. McGregor, Texas. October 16, 1998.

Pearsall, E. Robert. Interview with author. Abilene, Texas. June 8, 1998.

Pecos Army Air Field 1998 Reunion Booklet. Pecos (TX): *Pecos Enterprise*, 1998.

Pecos Enterprise: December 19, 1941; September 11, 1942; October 8, 1998.

Pitner, Jean B. "Project of the Community of Waco Air Force Base," Paper, Baylor University, 1949.

Pitts, Bill. Interview with author. Pecos, Texas. October 3, 1998.

Pool, William C. "The Origin of Military Aviation in Texas, 1910-1913." *Southwestern Historical Quarterly* LVII, No. 3, (January 1955).

Pringle, Art. Telephone interview with author. October 30, 1998.

Putnam, Harry G. Interview with author. Midland, Texas. August 12, 1998.

Radley, Thomas K. Interview with author. Harlingen, Texas. October 28, 1998.

Raimond, Vance Delone. *Transportation: Key to the Magic Valley*. Edinburg (TX): Santander Press, 1996.

Randolph, Ellen. "Randolph, The West Point of the Air." Unpublished essay, 1930.

Rogers, Mary Beth, Sherry A. Smith, and Janelle D. Scott. *We Can Fly: Stories of Katherine Stinson and Other Gutsy Texas Women*. Austin: Ellen C. Temple, Publisher, 1983.

San Angelo Standard-Times, February 16, 1964.

San Antonio Express, June 20, 1930.

San Antonio Express-News, September 8, 1994.

San Antonio Light: June 20, 1930; June 21, 1930; April 9, 1938; October 13, 1942; November 8, 1945.

Selvaggi, Rossi L. "A History of Randolph Air Force Base." Master's thesis, University of Texas, 1958.

Simpson, Arnold Frank. Interview with author. Abilene, Texas. June 9, 1998.

Slocum, Everett G. Interview with author. New Braunfels, Texas. September 12, 1998.

Steinbeck, John. *Travels With Charley.* New York: Penguin Books, 1986.

Stephens, A. Ray and William M. Holmes. *Historical Atlas of Texas.* Norman: University of Oklahoma Press, 1989.

Swanborough, Gordon and Peter M. Bowers. *United States Military Aircraft Since 1909.* Washington, D.C.: Smithsonian Institution Press, 1989.

Sweetwater Reporter: June 28, 1942; August 15, 1942; May 21, 1993.

Tanner, Doris Brinker, comp. *Who Were the WASP?* Sweetwater (TX): The *Sweetwater Daily Reporter,* 1989.

Texas Almanac and State Industrial Guide, 1939-40. Dallas: A. H. Belo Corporation, 1939.

Texas Almanac and State Industrial Guide, 1943-44. Dallas: A. H. Belo Corporation, 1943.

Texas Almanac and State Industrial Guide, 1994-1995. Dallas: *The Dallas Morning News,* 1993.

Timmons, Louise Marsh. Interview with author. Waco, Texas. October 17, 1998.

Tour of Historic Randolph. San Antonio: Office of History and Research, HQ Air Education and Training Command, 1996.

Tudor, William G. "Flight Of Eagles: The Mexican Expeditionary Air Force 'Escuadron' 201 In World War II." Ph.D. diss., Texas Christian University, 1997.

Tyler, Ron, ed. *The New Handbook of Texas.* 7 vols. Austin: The Texas State Historical Association, 1996.

Valley Morning Star: April 12, 1938; February 1, 1941; November 12, 1960; June 20, 1963; July 30, 1964; August 12, 1997.

Veit, Richard J., ed. *Waco Goes to War.* Waco (TX): Historic Waco Foundation, 1991.

Verges, Marianne. *On Silver Wings: The Women Airforce Service Pilots.* New York: Ballantine Books, 1991.

Waco Herald-Tribune: December 19, 1941; March 4, 1965.

Wagner, Ray. *American Combat Planes.* Garden City (NY): Doubleday & Company, Inc., 1982.

Wallace, Everett G. Interview with author. San Antonio, Texas. December 15, 1998.

Wallace, Patricia Ward. *Our Land, Our Lives: A Pictorial History of McLennan County.* Waco (TX): Waco Herald Tribune, 1976.

"Welcome to Harlingen." Harlingen (TX): Harlingen Chamber of Commerce Bulletin, October 7, 1947.

Westermann, Lloyd P. Interview with author. Amarillo, Texas. October 8, 1998.

Wheatley, John R. "The Economic Impact of Closing James Connally Air Force Base on the Waco Area." Master's thesis, Baylor University, 1966.

Willenz, June A. *Women Veterans: America's Forgotten Heroines.* New York: The Continuum Publishing Company, 1983.

Wolk, Herman S. *U.S. Air Force General Histories: Planning And Organizing The Postwar Air Force, 1943-1947.* Washington, D.C.: Office of Air Force History, 1984.

Yeats, E. L. and Hooper Shelton. *History of Nolan County, Texas.* Sweetwater (TX): Shelton Press, 1975.

Yenne, Bill. *The History of the United States Air Force.* New York: Exeter Books, 1984.

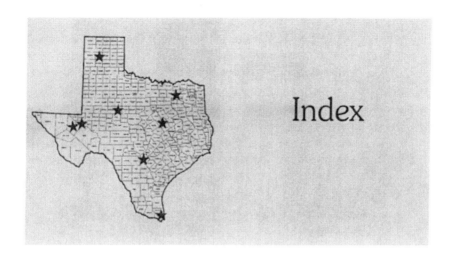

Index

B-17, 46, 56, 58, 59, 104, 176, 177, 178, 180, 196, 228-229
B-24, 164, 229, 232
B-25, 180, 205
B-29, 46, 60, 74, 131, 179, 180, 201, 229-230
B-34, 164
B-37, 164
B-47, 62
B-50, 131
B-52, 62, 78
B-57, 131
Baptist churches, 7
Baylor University, 105, 143, 147
"Baylor Victory, The," 147
BC-1, 236
Bean, Ariel F., 22
Belcher, George F. (Bud), 51
Bergstrom Field, 212
Berry, J. T., 53
Bexar County, 11, 111, 117, 119, 207
Bexar, Siege of, 111
Big Spring Army Air Field, 212
Big Spring, Texas, 26, 48
Biggs Field, 212
Black, Edward C. "Red," 58, 59
Blackburn, W. T., 55-56, 57, 58, 60
Blackland Army Air Field, 103, 212
Blue Laws, 44
"Bobcat," 230-231
Boeing, 228, 229
Bonham Municipal Airport, 212
bootleggers, 91
Borland, G. William, 127
Bostrom, Frank P., 180
Bradford, Louise, 41
Brooks Field, 116, 117, 118, 120, 125, 212
Brown, Stan, 25
Brownlee, Marian Harris, 92
Brownsville Herald, 159
Brownsville Municipal Airport, 212
Brownwood Army Air Field, 212
Bruce Field, 213

Bryan Army Air Field, 212
BT-13, 92, 141
buffalo hunters, 29, 31
Bulge, Battle of, 179
Burgesses, 115
Bushey, Orin J., 24
Butterfield-Overland Stage Route, 17

C

C-47, 180
Calf Hill, 119
Camacho, Avila, 93
Cameron County, 158, 160, 207
Cameron, Kate, 164
Camp Claiborne, Louisiana, 60
Campbell, H. O., 156
Caplinder, W. A. (Cap), 86, 90-91
Carlsbad, New Mexico, 26
Catholic churches, 7
cattle trails, 128
Celeste, Texas, 89
Cessna, 230-231
Chanute Field, 58
Chapin, Joe, 105, 146
Cheatham, C. F., 122-123
Chennault, Claire L., 32
Childress Army Air Field, 212
"City of Waco, Texas, The," 145
civil defense plans, 99-101
Civil Aeronautics Administration (CAA), 8-10, 33, 87, 162, 174
Civil War, 5, 85, 112, 160
Clark, Harold, 121-122, 151, 152, 153, 156
Clingan, Wilbur L. (Wib), 21
Coahuila y Tejas, 111
Cochran, Jacqueline, 38, 44
Cole, Emily Turner, 36-37
Coleman Flying School, 212
College Park, Maryland, 115
Confederate States of America, 5, 85, 112, 160
Connally Air Force Base, *also see* Waco Air Force Base and James Connally Air Force Base

Pecos Chamber of Commerce, 18, 19, 22, 27
Pecos City Council, 20, 27
Pecos Fire Department, 27, 67
Pecos Municipal Airport, 27
Pecos River, 17
Pecos, Texas, 15-28, 64-67, 130, 208, 209
Pecos Valley Country Club, 27
Pennsylvania Air National Guard, 237
Perrin Field, 213
Pershing, John J., 115
Peruvian national airline, 40
Philippine insurrection, 113
Philippines, 177, 180, 234
Phillips, Howard, 236
Pine, William, 164
Pitts, Bill, 23-24
Ploesti, Rumania, 232
Plosser and Prince Air Academy, 34-36
Pocatello, Idaho, 94
Post, Wiley, 32
Potter County, 52
Pounds Field, 213
Pringle, Art, 171
PT-1, 233
PT-3, 126
PT-13, 70, 163
PT-19, 42, 235-236
PT-23, 235
PT-26, 236
P-47, 47
Punitive Expedition, 115
Putnam, Harry G., 173
Pyote Army Air Field, 171-182, 192-203, 213, 220
Pyote, Texas, 130, 171-182, 191-203, 208

R
Rabaul, New Guinea, 177
race relations, 85-86, 91-92, 94, 96-97, 206
radar defense system, 49

railroad, 160, 172
Ramsey, Hugh, 162
Randolph Air Force Base, 2, 208
Randolph Auxiliary (Cade Field), 222
Randolph Auxiliary (Davenport Field), 223
Randolph Auxiliary (Krueger Field), 224
Randolph Auxiliary (Martindale Field), 225
Randolph Auxiliary (Zuehl Field), 226
Randolph Field, 3, 11, 93, 116-132, 150-157, 213, 221, 237
Randolph Field Cadet Guidebook, 129
Randolph, B. D., 129
  Ellen, 124, 125, 154
  Mrs. William M., 124
  William M., 122, 124, 151, 154
Rantoul, Illinois, 58
Ratliff, Harvey, 162
Rattlesnake Bomber Base, 171-182, 192-203
rattlesnakes, 21
Rayburn, Sam, 87, 88, 95-96
Raytheon Corporation, 96, 137
Reconstruction, 5
Reeves County, 14, 17, 19, 20
Republic Aviation Corporation, 238
Republic P-47 Thunderbolt, 47, 92, 135
Richards, Ann, 50
Richey, Helen, 40
Rio Grande, 159-160, 161
Rio Grande Valley, 160, 164, 167-169
Rio Grande Valley International Airport, 168
Rio Grande Valley Museum, 168
Rittiman, William, 119
Roosevelt, Franklin D., 8, 10, 13, 34, 178
  Theodore, 113

Printed in the United States
202760BV00004B/109-261/P